HOW TO RETURN TO WORK IN AN OFFICE

How to Return to Work in an Office

Mary Ralston
with Wilbur Cross

1817

Harper & Row, Publishers
New York, Evanston, San Francisco, London

STANDARD BOOK NUMBER: 06-013468-2

LIBRARY OF CONGRESS CATALOG CARD NUMBER: 72-79689

Acknowledgments

My thanks go to Al P. Nelson, free-lance writer and writing instructor at the University of Wisconsin Extension, who suggested I write this book and gave me much help and encouragement; to my sister, Flora McEachern; to the First Wisconsin National Bank of Milwaukee, especially Ann Judith Neville, who worked as my assistant while I was Assistant Personnel Director there, and to the bank's head librarians, Evelyn M. Tessman and Mildred Jones and their staffs; to Elizabeth Duncan Koontz, Deputy Assistant Secretary and Director of the Women's Bureau; to Sister Joel Read, President, Alverno College; to Sister Mary Austin Doherty, Chairman of the Psychology Department, Alverno College; to Anne Thorsen Truax, Director, Minnesota Planning and Counseling Center for Women, University of Minnesota; Mrs. Virgil Arrowood, Counselor, Hibbing State Junior College, Hibbing, Minn.

Thanks also to Martha S. Luck, Dean, Evening Divisions, Northwestern University, Chicago, Illinois; to Helen Alexander, Child Development Administrator, Day Care Services for Children, Inc.; to Dr. Raymond J. McCall, Professor of Psychology, Marquette University; to Professor Dorothy E. Miniace, Director Continuing Education, University of Wisconsin, Milwaukee; to Carol L. Hull, Executive Director, Career Clinic for Mature Women, Inc., Minneapolis, Minn.; to Catherine Conroy, International Representative, Communications Workers of America, Affiliated with AFL-CIO; to James M. Cotterell, Area Manager, Milwaukee Area Office,

U.S. Civil Service Commission; to Mary Bresnahan, State Women's Employment Specialist, Wisconsin State Employment Service; to Anita M. Kearin, Director, Federal Information Center, General Services Administration, Region 5, Chicago, Illinois; to Erna K. Carmichael, Consumer Marketing Agent, Milwaukee County Extension Office, University of Wisconsin; to Ardie Halyard, Chairman of the Board, Columbia Savings and Loan Association; to Barbara Andrews, Assistant Director of Management and Personnel Development, Employers Insurance of Wausau.

Many thanks to Carol Kleiman for permission to quote from "Working Woman," *Chicago Tribune*; to Enterprise Publications for permission to quote from "Listening Is a Ten Part Skill" by Dr. Ralph Nichols; to Warren T. Farrell for permission to quote from *Beyond Masculinity;* and to Harold D. Pletcher, Vice President, First National Bank of Chicago, for permission to quote material describing their Plan Ahead Center.

Grateful acknowledgment is made to the United States Civil Service Commission for permission to reprint the sample questions that appear on pages 219 to 224 in this book.

The housewife who goes back to work after a number of years of homemaking, or who decides to take a job for the first time, has an obligation to make the most of her capabilities. It isn't enough to settle into the first job that comes along. She may have to start at something that requires less than she is capable of doing but she should be alert to opportunities for training and advancement to something that will give her true satisfaction and an opportunity to make a full contribution to society.

—ELIZABETH DUNCAN KOONTZ
Deputy Assistant Secretary of Labor and
Director Women's Bureau
Employment Standards Administration
U.S. Department of Labor

Foreword

This is a book for the woman who has been considering returning to an office job. A former secretary, typist, or billing clerk, she is now perhaps a mother whose children have left home and who finds herself at loose ends, a woman who has become the main support of her family, a widow or divorcee who needs additional income, or a woman who wants to help educate her children. She is perhaps a wife who wants to move to a better neighborhood and is willing to help her husband in making this possible.

That she is there we know, for there are thousands of women joining the work force each year, many of them married women.

That she needs help we also know: first in making her decision to return to work and secondly in discovering how to go about it.

During the past twenty years I have interviewed thousands of women who want to return to work, and it is my intention to provide a useful guidebook for those women.

M. R.

Contents

HOW TO RETURN TO WORK IN AN OFFICE

Chapter 1

Do You Want to Go Back to Work?

If you are like millions of women, you have a strong desire, and perhaps a pressing need, both to go back to work and to get the most you can out of work. And yet other people may be holding you back, either consciously or not, by repeating in one way or another that tired, outmoded idea that "a woman's place is in the home."

"Tradition"—that word is often a poor excuse for resisting change and doing something positive about your life. When you hear the phrase, "But it's always been this way," be careful! If you examine the facts you will often find that, although there once was a real reason for doing something a certain way, that reason no longer exists. Let me illustrate.

A new husband I heard about was recently amazed to see his bride trying to saw off the protruding bone on a ham she wanted to bake.

"Why do you do that?" he asked.

"I don't know. My mother always did."

The curious husband asked his mother-in-law, who told him *her* mother had always done this.

Still curious, he questioned his mother-in-law's eighty-five-year-old mother. She said, "I always sawed the bone off because the pan was too short."

When it comes to women going back to work, many people are still sawing away at bones when the short pan has long since been replaced.

1

During the years I worked as a personnel executive, I interviewed thousands and thousands of housewives who wanted to go back to work, and I know the difficulties you face.

Why Do Women Work?

When you hear people say, "Woman's place is in the home," remind them that women live very much longer than they used to. Generations ago women did not live long enough to be any place much except the home. If you take a walk through an old cemetery, you may see something like this: Angus McGeachie, died age fifty-six. Lined up beside old Angus may be as many as three graves. Eliza, beloved wife of Angus, died age twenty-two. Then there is Sarah, died age twenty-six. Hannah, died age twenty-nine. So many women died in childbirth then that if a woman lived to be forty she was considered an "old" woman.

By 1900 a woman's life expectancy had increased to forty-eight years; in 1920, to fifty-five years. Now the average woman may live to be seventy-five. By the time a woman of today is forty, therefore, she may still have thirty to thirty-five productive years ahead of her.

After you've blown out forty candles on your birthday cake, your next step certainly does not have to be down the road to oblivion. One woman said to me, "When I kissed my daughter good-bye and sent her off to college, I looked at myself and said, 'You're forty. Now what are you going to do with the rest of your life?' "

That is what many women are asking.

When I interviewed these thousands of housewives, some young and some middle-aged, some widowed and some divorced, some very poor and some not poor at all, they had one thing in common: Although many of them could easily find jobs, they did not always do so, because *they were afraid to take the step.*

The reasons were much the same.

"Well, I've been thinking of taking a job for more than a year now," said thirty-eight-year-old Marie Johnson, bored by inactivity at home, "but I'm too nervous about going back to an office. I haven't even been in one for sixteen years. I wouldn't know what to do."

"I want to work for the money we need to pay overflow bills and for something to do now that my boys are in college," said another typical job applicant, "but I'm forty-seven and I can't face the idea of going in for an interview with personnel managers and trying to compete with all those pretty young girls just out of school."

"I wish my mother would get a job," said the daughter of a recent widow. "She spends all her time moping, crying, and living in the past. She expects my husband and me to take her on all our vacations. She never makes any plans for herself. She'd be so much better off making a life for herself with new interests and a job, rather than trying to live through her children, who are all grown up now."

This is what happens to countless widows who thought their only career would be that of wife and mother. Their whole lives have been merely an extension of the lives of their husbands and children. Nursing homes are full of lonely elderly women who believed that their only career would be that of a wife and mother. Or perhaps these elderly women are like those who spend many of their days in such places as department store lounges. One such woman said, "Old people have to go some place. We can't just sit home and look out of the window." Another said, "We are widows who have to watch our pennies. We depend on our husband's social security and it isn't enough, but we don't want to die in a nursing home." They think a lot about what it means to get old and be alone, without much money. The department store rest room is more cheerful than sitting alone at home.

One widow who broke through the barriers and did go back to work said, "I have a whole new outlook on life. I'm proud that I'm not a burden to my children. I enjoy seeing them, but I don't hang on their coattails as so many widows do. So they enjoy seeing me, too."

You might be surprised to know how many grandmothers there are who go back to work successfully. Grandmothers want jobs, not only for extra money which they need when no longer living with children, but for outside contacts and something worthwhile to occupy their time. Since this country is continually on the move —today, some 40 million people move from one location to another—in the process many physically fit grandmothers find themselves alone as sons and daughters change jobs or are promoted to better ones elsewhere. Also, since community and family life do not have the closeness they once had, older people are more detached from the various members of their family than they once were. Years ago, there was usually a spare bedroom for grandma. Now there rarely is.

Younger married women, too, often find themselves in strange communities where their husbands' transfers have taken them. I interviewed a young woman in this situation, and at first glance I wondered why she wanted to go back to work. Her husband held a good position, made an excellent salary, and they had a young son. "We won't be in this city more than a year and a half," she said, "which isn't long enough to put your roots down and make fast friends. And anyway, I'm not the 'clubwoman' type. Also, my little boy is very lonesome. He'd be much happier during the day in a nursery school where he'd have other children his age to play with. As for me, I'd be much happier, too, in an office where I had plenty to do and some adult companionship during the day."

We condemn far too many young mothers for wanting to get out of the house. For one thing, a child should not be solely the mother's responsibility. For another, in an earlier day, a young mother lived in what we now call "the extended family," with grandparents, aunts, uncles, cousins, even domestic help to give the young mother a hand. And it can be a very lonely life for a young couple with small children, especially in a big city.

Whenever I talk with young women, I wish that more of them realize what the statistics show: that women work now on the average of twenty-five years of their lives. Too many girls assume that marriage will automatically end their participation in the work force. A great deal of that is society's fault. We condition girls from childhood on to think that being a wife and mother is all they will ever be.

Since one out of four marriages ends in divorce, many young women, and older ones, too, are plunged suddenly back into the working world whether they like it or not. When I interviewed housewives, I observed that, of the divorced ones, many were very young. It was not unusual to interview a woman of twenty-one who was already divorced and had two children to support.

Then there were the divorcees in their early forties. Many of them had married very young, during World War II. One who had been married twenty-five years told me, "I was devastated. I felt so inadequate. Like a complete zero. Then I got a job where people told me I did well. I began to feel dignified and important. It was a wonderful thing to feel like a person, a real human being again."

If you are a divorcee, you may like to know that a clinical psychologist has said that taking a job is better than rushing into a second marriage. In addition to bringing in money (for it was my observation that many women found it difficult to get the support payments), a job can help restore your confidence and build up your ego. And it can often help greatly in enlarging your circle of friends, both male and female.

There still persist some myths about women working that I shall try to clear up throughout the book.

Myth: Women are taking jobs away from men.

"My biggest hangup," admitted Linda Reynolds, whose husband was having a desperate time trying to keep up the mortgage payments and take care of unexpected maintenance costs on a new home, "is what the neighbors will think. Or my parents, who are very critical about women who work. You still read about unemployed men, and I'm not sure it's right for me to take a job."

The reality: The nation's unemployment figures can sometimes present a misleading picture. On April 27, 1972, *The Wall Street Journal* wrote, "Unemployment is high, but many good jobs are awaiting takers. Experts blame lack of data and workers' reluctance to move to new locations." The article went on to explain that these vacancies were not for menial jobs, such as emptying bedpans or digging ditches, but were rather for jobs that could be done by highly skilled workers. And since many of the unemployed are those who are either unskilled or else overqualified for some office jobs, it stands to reason that you cannot successfully fill a stenographer's job if you are an unskilled day laborer or a physicist with a Ph.D.

It is well to keep in mind that during a recession many a man has been thankful his wife has a job, so he can have some time to look for another position. It has been a new experience for many men to be without a job; this new generation of men being laid off really never had much trouble getting jobs. With a wife working, the family situation did not seem quite so desperate until the man could find another job.

The Women's Bureau, United States Department of Labor, points out how dramatically women's work-life patterns have changed since 1920, the year the Women's Bureau was founded.

In 1920 the average woman worker was single and twenty-eight years old. Today 60 percent of women workers are married, and the average is thirty-nine years old. In 1920 the 8.2 million women workers had very few job choices. Today there are over 31 million women workers, comprising almost 40 percent of the entire labor force, who are needed in many different kinds of jobs.

You may recall "Rosie the Riveter," who during World War II produced whistles, stares, and wolf calls at the same time she was helping produce airplanes. In that important era in our history women were badly needed in the work force, and in great numbers. Yet today more women are working than ever was the case during World War II.

What about the problems and limitations caused by having a family and children? Well, this apparently is not as much of a restriction as one might think. Of those 31 million working women, more than 10 million are mothers with children who are under eighteen. And of these mothers, more than 4 million have children six years or younger. So it does seem feasible and realistic for women to combine family life with outside work. But it is not always easy for women with young children who absolutely *must* work. I cannot repeat often enough the desperate need for more day care centers.

Many Women Have to Work

The myth that enrages women: Women are just temporary workers; they're just working for pin money.

The reality: United States Department of Labor statistics show that of the more than 31 million women in the labor force, nearly half are working because of pressing economic need. For many families, the wife's income makes the difference between poverty and scraping by.

In addition, millions of women are heads of households. In 1972 women headed one out of nine families in the United States.

The woman may be the sole wage earner due to widowhood, divorce, or having a disabled husband with not enough pension or other income to support a family. And with the tragedy of three wars involving the United States in the past thirty years, many such families can be found.

Income levels for 17 percent of white women household heads in 1970 were below the poverty level of $4,000 for an urban family of four, but hardest hit of all were minority women household heads, with 40 percent of their number below the $4,000 poverty level for an urban family of four.

There are over 8 million widows in the United States, a number that has gone up by almost a million in the last five years alone. Many widows are forced to work, with more than half of those over thirty-five holding a job or looking for one. If you are a widow in the thirty-five to fifty-four age bracket, almost two-thirds of you are dependent on a job. Unhappily, the average man lives about seven years less than the average woman.

There are many *young* widows, too. I recall a fine young stenographer who came to say good-bye because her husband had found a better-paying job in another city. The next day she received word that he had been killed in an automobile accident. She had not intended to keep on working, but there was little choice for her after this tragedy—which was by no means unique. Thousands of women are made widows through automobile accidents, and if you add these to the other thousands who lost husbands in the three recent wars, you have a sizable population of women who are on their own because they have to be. And even when a young widow does not really need a job in order to survive, she may feel like one who said to me, "Every woman, no matter what her situation, has to have a corner of the world that is just hers."

Women also go back to work to provide benefits for the family. Only a second income makes possible houses and college educations for many families. In 1971 a federal study showed it costs the average American family nearly $40,000 to rear a child from birth through college, but with inflation that figure goes out of date so fast all one can say is, "This is an expensive undertaking. The costs go up and up." Many wives feel this is too much of a burden for a man to assume without her help.

Women work, too, because health care costs more, and many families have to face huge medical and health bills for relatives who are chronically ill, deformed, or handicapped. Other women work to assist aged parents in maintaining a home, or to provide nursing care in a rest home.

The cost of equipment, automobiles, music lessons, travel, goods, and services to meet the American standard of living make many women want to contribute to the family's needs. Another common situation is that of the woman who is growing older, has a working husband, but who wants to help with retirement plans. The couple can see that while their current income is comfortable, inflation and unexpected expenses can take a heavy toll of their retirement dollars.

Money Is Not the Only Reason for Going Back to Work

Economic reasons chiefly motivate a woman's desire to return to work, but other reasons are emerging.

Congress has pressed the rehabilitation services administration in the Department of Health, Education and Welfare for action on what it regards as a growing problem—female alcoholic addiction.

According to testimony at the 1969 hearings, the most "startling" development of the last several years is the increased incidence of female alcoholics among lonely suburban housewives in the forty to fifty age bracket.

A suburban housewife, not herself an alcoholic, wrote to the chairman of the hearings to say that too many successful men don't want their wives to work for fear it will lower their prestige! She said her husband did not admit to anyone for nearly a year that she had taken a part-time job. Then, one evening when he told her a friend's wife was an alcoholic and another was getting a divorce, she reminded him how many times he had told her similar stories —and it was only then that he realized at all why she had wanted to go back to work. For many women, with children in school, the house is very lonely from 8:30 A.M. to 3:30 P.M. five days a week, nine months a year. Many women, who may have held volunteer jobs for years, are tired of them. Others are tired of bridge and similar activities, so some fill the hours with drink. But those who do manage to go back to work find it gives them a whole new lease on life.

Some of the men who have been critical of women going back to work concentrate their fire on the suburban housewife because they claim she is giving up her responsibilities. But some of the women have begun to fight back.

"I took a part-time job," said one of them to me, "to get away from the endless kaffeeklatching about husbands, kids, the neighbors, and other gossip."

Another told me with a somewhat bitter laugh, "Sure I was the Big Wheel of the family—the chauffeur, at everyone's beck and call. It got so no one could go anywhere on foot or on the bus as long as I was around. I finally checked the car mileage and was shocked to find that I was *averaging fifty-six miles a day* taxiing four children, and sometimes their friends, in addition to driving my husband to and from the train. Now I work part time, have money for extras, and everyone seems to get where he wants to be without having a personal chauffeur. I figure I'm helping ecology, too, because bikes are popular once more."

You Won't Feel Like an Odd Duck in the Employment Pool

Many middle-aged women have reached that period in life when they have what noted poet T. S. Eliot called "the Hoo-ha's." These are vague fears that many of us have about this and that, and often nothing in particular.

As I mentioned before, many of you who are interested in going back to work are timid about getting out of the house and trying to compete with the young things you picture as making up the entire office force.

The actual picture is much different.

I wish you could see how much younger, more attractive, and more vivacious the average housewife looks after *she has gone back to work*! The change is often remarkable, so much so that many more of you would make the step toward going back to work if you could foresee the results.

The average housewife or any woman who formerly worked does get butterflies when she thinks about getting back into the employment stream. She needs a great deal of reassurance. Yet I know from experience, and from the experiences of my colleagues in the personnel field, that most women make the transition rather easily once they make up their minds to go ahead.

You may well ask, as others have over and over again, "But *where* do I start? *What* can I do? Who would want me? What will my husband, children, and friends think?" And if you are thirty-five or forty, maybe fifty or older, you may ask, "What chance do I have against all the competition?"

These figures may reassure you. The woman most likely to be in the labor force today is aged forty-five to fifty-four. Almost half the married women that age are working or looking for work. And at the ages of fifty-five to sixty-four, over a third are employed. As the Institute of Life Insurance reports, every year, mature women reenter the labor force or join it for the first time.

I do not want to make it sound too easy for every woman to return to work successfully. For some it is difficult, if not impossible. But in interviewing thousands of housewives who want to go back to work in an office (or elsewhere), I have learned there are all kinds of ways most women can accomplish this. There are many ways in which you can help yourself, find new interests, supplement your present income, and get more enjoyment and satisfaction out of life.

Lack of confidence is probably one of the greatest barriers most housewives face when they think about going back to work, so in the next chapter we shall explore some practical and proven ways to build confidence and take a positive and constructive approach.

Chapter 2

Building Your Confidence— an Important Step

Now it is time to ask yourself some questions—not in a negative way, but to help you establish your aims and point you in the right direction. This is an important step in establishing your self-assurance.

Why do you want to go back to work?

Do you want to work for just a short period of time, or over a period of some years?

Do you want a full-time job, or would you prefer shorter hours?

What do the key members of your family think about the idea of your going back to work?

It is very important, especially in building your own self-confidence, to get the family on your side and have them appreciate your viewpoint. Filling two jobs—that of a housewife and that of an employee—is not an easy task to begin with. To do it successfully takes a certain amount of family cooperation and help. It is equally important for the members of your family to realize, every step of the way, just how much the life styles for women have changed in the past few decades.

Just take a look at the change in attitudes, for example, since the end of World War II. Before the war it was the young girl—usually the single girl—who was most often looking for work. Young girls worked for a few years in an office before they married, but then dropped quickly out of the work force with the characteristic comment, "My husband doesn't want me to work."

Jobs then were also very, very scarce.

Those were the days when many firms would not employ married women, or did so reluctantly when they could not find replacements from the ranks of the single. So by the time most women reached the age bracket of thirty-five to fifty-four, their chances of finding a job were slim. Indeed, many ads stated "Wanted: Young single girl not over 25." Advertising like this today would violate fair employment practice laws. And *since there are more than twice as many office jobs now as there were in 1940,* an office would find it difficult, if not impossible, to fill all jobs with young single girls.

The year after the war ended, 1946, more than half the World War II veterans went back to college or to some kind of training school under the GI Bill. That year also marked the all-time high in the United States marriage rate. Many young wives took jobs to support their GI husbands. Ph.T. (pushing hubby through) was the degree many girls received then, many of them dropping their own college plans to become the family's provider. (This, incidentally, changed some of the old conservative male attitude that married women should not work). Many of these couples have celebrated their twenty-fifth anniversaries, and the Ph.T. wives are the very ones who are now thinking about going back to work. Some are thinking, too, about going back to college to get their own degrees. Over four hundred fifty colleges and universities have plans and counseling for mature women who want to do this. We shall discuss this in a later chapter.

We have seen how World War II brought many demands for women workers because of the simple fact that the United States could not have met its defense efforts if women had not been recruited for the work force and then showed a willingness to venture into unfamiliar worlds of employment. Many doors, long closed to women, suddenly opened. A few closed again right after the war, but for the most part they, along with new ones, have opened. And one of the greatest changes since World War II is the fact that, for the first time in our history, office jobs outnumber factory jobs.

Recent Laws Help Women

We who work know full well that it is very important that out-moded attitudes about women employees be changed. A chairman of the United States Industrial Commission has said, "There must be a realization that equal opportunity is not a favor to women, but an economic necessity." Noting that women make up almost 40 percent of the nation's labor force, he added, "The fact is that the high levels of economic activity we now enjoy cannot be maintained without the extensive employment of women, both in government and in industry."

The Equal Pay Act of 1963 prohibits discrimination in pay on the basis of the sex of the workers.

Title VII of the Civil Rights Act of 1964 applies to all phases of employment, prohibits discrimination because of race, color, religion, sex, or national origin.

The Age Bias law passed in June 1967 prohibits discrimination against those in the forty to sixty-five age bracket.

Revised Order 4, which became effective April 3, 1972, will be described in detail in a later chapter.

In addition, in recent years there have been a growing number of aids to help the housewife who wants to return to work.

The Back-to-Work Clinics

Various sponsors, such as churches, Chambers of Commerce, temporary help placement services, the YWCA, and others have encouraged housewives with such clinics.

Notable among them have been those sponsored by the YWCA. Since 1961 the Central YWCA, 37 South Wabash Avenue, Chicago, Illinois, has done an outstanding job in presenting a back-to-work symposium for women over thirty-five. The all-day session always includes a panel of women who did go back to work, and who discuss how they went about getting their jobs and who hired them. They point out, as well, some of the disappointments and barriers to overcome.

In this same symposium a specialist discusses the job interview; a panel from business and industry describe the job possibilities in their fields of work; and another speaker tells how to put your best foot forward, stressing good grooming, good health habits, the right clothes, and the discipline to gain self-confidence.

You might try asking at your local YWCA to see if they have such clinics, or write to the National Board YWCA, 600 Lexington Avenue, New York, N.Y. 10022 to find out what other Y's have programs similar to the one in Chicago.

Watch your newspapers for announcements about back-to-work clinics, especially in early fall and sometimes in January.

Career Clinic for Mature Women, Inc.

Nannette Jayne Elmquist, who conceived the idea for the Career Clinic for Mature Women, Inc., in 1958, hadn't worked full time since her marriage thirty years earlier. This agency has had remarkable success in counseling and qualifying mature women for productive and profitable employment, training about three hundred women annually.

Mrs. Elmquist retired in 1970. Carol L. Hull, now the executive director, has some encouraging words for you. Says Mrs. Hull, "Strangely, this winter session (1972) is the first time we have failed to fill both afternoon and evening classes. I think that this may be a negative response from the women because they think, 'With unemployment so bad, why take the training when I probably won't even find a job.' *Not true*.

"We have had an unusual number of employment agencies calling us in the past several months pleading for us to ask our students to register with them. Clerical jobs come into these agencies and they can't fill them. If you read our guidebook, you will be amazed at the opportunities that have opened to our women, even now in this economic situation."

This surely illustrates that many job seekers give up too soon.

The clinic offers a refresher course in typing and other skills seven times a year and other courses, too. To obtain further information write Mrs. Carol L. Hull, Executive Director, 127 City Hall, Minneapolis, Minn. 55415.

Federal Aid for Job Training

For the woman who can't afford brush-up courses, there is federal aid. In a later chapter, I shall write in detail about where to find job leads, and especially about state employment services. There you will find counselors who can tell you about the various federal programs.

Housewives Must Help Themselves, Too

All of the foregoing efforts do much to get the mature woman into the swing of going back to work. However, one fact that comes out in the back-to-work clinics and elsewhere is that, while many middle-aged housewives sincerely *want* to go back to work, sometimes they are just not willing to make some of the adjustments needed. Some say they would love to take additional training, but they have just planned a vacation trip and cannot start in a class when it opens in September or whenever. Or they use the excuse that the class comes on the same day as bowling and/or bridge.

As one woman said, "Well, if I get a good job, I'll brush up my typing, reduce, and do something about my hair."

The time to do all these things is *before* you even go to apply for a job, or you may be sadly disappointed.

When a woman has been away from an office for some years, she really needs some brushup of office skills if only to give her confidence. She may have been a whiz on the typewriter twenty years ago, but is scared to death of using an electric typewriter now, to say nothing of her fears about computers and the younger miniskirted competition.

Like many others I'd advise you to take the brushup course, if you possibly can, before you even start looking for a job.

Chapter 3

Advance Planning
You Can Do at Home

What do women say when someone talks to them about job opportunities and preparing to go back to work? There are some women who say, "Why don't you leave us alone?" "We are perfectly happy and content just to stay at home," "My husband doesn't want me to work," or "I love being on a pedestal." In answer to that, one divorced woman said, "Well, the trouble with making your whole life being an adornment on a pedestal is that you may find yourself, along about forty-five, being changed for a younger model. And there you are not knowing how to make a life for yourself, or how to earn a living." Another woman said, "I don't understand women who say 'Oh, but it wouldn't be feminine to do a man's work!' My great-grandmother wouldn't know what to make of these modern hangups of what is feminine and what is masculine. If she hadn't known how to shoot straight and hadn't had enough sense to grab the rifle and take a shot at marauders near the wilderness cabin, she and her family would never have survived."

Every woman ought to know how to earn her own living, and she should not wait until circumstances force her into the working world. Being prepared is a cushion for future shock.

Take a long-range view of your prospects. Ask yourself "Where do I want to be five or ten years from now? Why do I want this job?" If you are a widow or divorcee, are you thinking that a job will be just a time killer until "the right man comes along?" Do you want the job to meet a financial emergency, or do you want to use your training, your abilities to the fullest? A clear understanding of *why* you want your job will save mistakes and help you grow in the right direction because your job can mean more than just putting in time and drawing a salary.

I have had many interesting experiences in which I've hired the same women twice. The first time they were just out of high school, and their only thought was to work until marriage. Then they would retire forever, they thought, from what they considered monotonous work. The second time occurred when they were about thirty-five or forty years old. Then even the most routine office job seemed exciting compared with housework! This time around, though, they came with much higher goals in mind. They were interested in advancement opportunities, training classes, fringe benefits, and other such considerations.

When you start looking for a job after a lapse of some years, you will need to be realistic, and to analyze your skills and abilities before you can set out to sell them. Take stock of your assets. Think of yourself as an individual. How long has it been since you thought of yourself as anyone but Bill's wife, or Barbie's mother? Now think of *you*—a person about to make out a résumé.

Compiling Material for a Résumé

Not everyone agrees with me, but I recommend against sending out resumés in advance of job interviews when you've been away from the job market for a long time. For one thing, they often make you look older than you really are. Chronological age does not tell the whole story about women, or men either.

I have seen women in the teens or early twenties who were so listless and apathetic they seemed old far beyond their years. On the other hand, I've seen women in their forties, fifties, and older who have really contagious zest and enthusiasm, two traits highly desirable in employees. They seem much younger than they really are. And after I saw an attractive woman, well into her eighties, swing gracefully through a rumba on a cruise ship, I stopped evaluating women in terms of chronological years. Think about that when some paunchy thirty-year-old implies, "You're too old."

I do strongly recommend, though, that you make up a résumé at home, because it will help you search your memory in preparation for some of the questions interviewers will ask.

1. First, consider your education. How far did you go? Have you taken any courses since you were graduated from high school or college? It may help you decide the kind of job you want to prepare for if you try to think back about the courses you liked best and the ones you liked least.

Many women are embarrassed and feel inferior because they lack a college degree, yet degrees in themselves are seldom a sign of intellect or possession of knowledge. In a later chapter we'll discuss ways you can get advanced education if you want to.

2. Work experience and skills. List your previous jobs. Do try to recall some specific details about them. If you were a typist, how many words a minute can you type now? Do you have a typewriter at home? Have you ever used an electric typewriter? Did you ever do statistical typing? Statistical typists are in big demand. Since many young girls don't like this kind of work, an older woman who is a good statistical typist has a real advantage in the job market.

Did you have much public contact and telephone work in previous jobs? Did you ever use a switchboard or have telephone company training? The ability to handle telephone calls tactfully is a definite asset in any office. In many small offices, the receptionist and switchboard jobs are combined. Always mention any special equipment you used, even though it may be out of date now. Being able to use a variety of machines indicates that you are flexible. It is sad to observe the number of women returning to work who never did anything but a little filing and light typing for perhaps a year before marriage. These are the women who especially need to learn the whole new world of office machines today.

3. In addition to paid employment, be sure to list *volunteer* experience you have had. Civil service now gives credit for volunteer jobs held if you can list the work you have done and give the dates of your service, kinds of skills used, and references from the supervisor in charge.

In an excellent booklet, "Job Finding Techniques for Mature Women," the Women's Bureau, U.S. Department of Labor, has this to say about volunteer activities:

What skills did your volunteer activities call for? For example, a good committee chairman develops techniques in management, learns to supervise others effectively, and enhances her coordinating ability. Helping with fund raising activities develops skills in making contacts with people, meeting deadlines, and 'selling' the work of an agency to others. . . . Practically all volunteer activity has aspects that are assets in the job world, even if they only demonstrate a liking for people and an ability to work with them.

4. List any work you may have done in your husband's business. I have interviewed many a woman who never thought to mention this, until at the very end of the interview she might chance to say, "My husband had a small business. I pitched in to mail out monthly bills. I covered the office when no one else could be there, so I handled incoming telephone calls and contacts with customers. It was never a real job, yet there was hardly a month when I didn't help out somewhere."

Such a woman, of course, would know just what to anticipate in a "one-woman office" where one would be expected to handle many different jobs. There are many such small offices. Never underestimate the kind of training that has kept you current with the business world.

Writing the Résumé

The outline for a general résumé should be typed on 8½ x 11 white bond paper. Keep it as short as possible.

1. In the upper left corner list your name, address, telephone, and social security number.

2. In the upper right side indicate the type of work you want if, of course, you know this.

3. Then under Work Experience list your last three or four jobs in reverse order, beginning with your last job. Some people go too far back and list so many jobs that interviewers get tired reading about all of them. This can also make you look old and out of date. Stay as close to the present as possible.

4. State name, address, and telephone number of each company. Unfortunately, many companies go out of business or merge. In that case, find a manager who may recall your work. Again this is why it is so important to have that brushup course and a reference from your teachers.

5. Give dates of employment, and name and title of your supervisor. You would be amazed at the people who write dates worked "June until November," so you don't know whether they worked from June 1956 until November 1961, or whatever. Be sure to include the year.

6. Give title for each position you held and briefly describe your duties. Start each sentence with an active verb, such as "Took dictation at 80 words a minute," or "Used dictating machine," or "Performed key punch work," or "Operated switchboard and did receptionist work."

7. Education. List schools attended, dates, and principal subjects studied, as well as courses taken since graduation. Give the name of school or organization where you took your brushup course, name of teacher, telephone number, length of course, date of completion. Quite often, mention of this recent brushup course can be one of the most helpful things you have on your list, since it shows that you have worked with modern equipment and demonstrates your ambition to be up to date.

8. If they seem related to the job you're seeking, briefly list volunteer activities, giving:

    a. Name, address, and telephone number of the agency or institution.

    b. Dates you served.

    c. Duties performed.

    d. Name, address, telephone number, and title of agency officer familiar with your work.

9. Under personal information list:

    a. Date of birth (optional). If you are hired, you'll have to give it for social security records, but you needn't always put it on résumés, and in some states they don't ask for it on preliminary application blanks.

    b. Marital status and number of dependents, if any. Many

women are supporting in full, or in part, invalid husbands, children, or aged parents. Many younger women are helping to support husbands in college or graduate school.

c. Preferred geographic location.

d. If appropriate to the job, whether you are free to travel, whether you have a driver's license and a car.

10. Under Personal References, supply the name, address, telephone number, and position of two or three people who know you personally. Never use a name for personal reference without asking the person first.

By this time, you may be thinking about all sorts of things that may help you to prepare for a job.

To help you keep track of the various ideas you collect I'd suggest borrowing an idea from Al P. Nelson, noted free-lance writer and writing instructor at the University of Wisconsin Extension.

How to Build a Clipping File

Nelson recommends that all his students emulate "the writer who, with marking pencil handy, reads newspapers and magazines which will act as springboards for articles, stories, etc." You can do the same thing, clipping new ideas that will help find the job best for you. Nelson continues, "Mark with pencil or ink the complete articles or excerpts you wish to save as idea starters. Record on the clipping the name of the publication and the date."

"You need not buy filing folders," he continues. "I prefer old mailing envelopes. I can trim these folders to 9 x 12 inches or less, leaving two sides uncut, so clippings cannot easily slide out. In an ordinary manila folder, two sides and the top are open, and small clippings may slide out and get lost when you take the folders out of the file. Mark each folder exterior with the name of the classification you wish to use." Get a corrugated box from any market, cover it if you want to, and presto, you have an inexpensive filing system.

Most women never have time to keep notebooks, but in this way you can keep files, not only to help you find a job, but to help in home management.

You'll think of many subjects for your file, I'm sure, but as a starter you can have a file about possible job leads from studying the want ad section, salary ranges also from studying the want ad section, articles about firms moving to the suburbs or to your small town in the real estate section, articles on consumer education to help stretch your dollar, time-saving techniques in cooking, and articles about working women to give you moral support.

Some years ago I. A. R. Wylie wrote an article in *Harper's* magazine called *The Little Woman.* In it she said:

The famous jester, Joe Miller, probably under the influence of a Restoration banquet, once boasted that, at a moment's notice, he could make a joke on any subject. He was immediately challenged to make a joke about the King. As in those days jests about the monarchy was an unhealthy amusement, Mr. Miller had to think fast. "The King, gentlemen," he said, "is no subject."

And thereby won his bet and withdrew his neck to safety.

Contrariwise, Woman is always a subject. Whenever lecturers, essayists, psychoanalysts, or women themselves have nothing else to talk, write, or worry about, they can always propound such questions as "Do Women—?" "Why Don't Women—?" or "Are Women—?" and find an audience, if no answers. It would seem that Woman, by accepted tradition, is always a woman before she is anything else, in counter-distinction to a man who may be first and foremost a plumber or a poet.

It would seem that even today many fancy themselves amateur psychiatrists when it comes to Woman, making her a chronic interrogation mark and never thinking of her as a person, as Man is. Therefore it was really a delight to discover a column called "Working Woman" in the Chicago *Tribune.* Carol Kleiman wrote about women as individual persons as they live in the world today. Here is an excerpt from the initial column as it appeared May 28, 1967:

Everyone talks about the working woman, but nobody knows her name. She's been put under a microscope and dissected by the experts. She's been told to stay home and do the dishes. And then she's been told she can have any career she wants if only she lets herself have one.

Everyone talks to the working woman. Everyone has advice. But nobody lets her answer. Meanwhile, millions of young, single women work. So do married women with or without children. And thousands of mature women enter the labor market each year and start working for the first time in their lives or for the first time in years.

This is unique. It's a revolution in the work force and in equality for women, and all working women—you and I—are caught up in it. We have problems, and we have possibilities. . . .

In the ensuing columns, Carol Kleiman has discussed many of the problems and successes working women have. Women write to her, too.

This illustrates some of the changes that have taken place in what used to be called the "women's pages" in daily newspapers. Women still like to read about fashion and food, but many women journalists now say that the work of the women's section reporter is more challenging and stimulating than it has been in the past because their work must reflect the much broader range of interests women have today.

Said one woman journalist, "We examine our pages now to be sure they reach a wide variety of readers—the working women of all races, the teenager, the elderly, the divorcee, and men, too." Indeed, some newspapers now call what used to be women's pages "family pages."

You will find, too, that now more newspapers and some magazines have columns called "Where the Jobs Are," "You and Your Job," "Women Who Work," "For the Working Woman," to name some in addition to the one mentioned above.

Moreover, some business magazines and business newspapers now actively look for women readers. On August 24, 1972, one of the major business magazines had an ad in the *New York Times* where it announced it had three million women readers. A major business newspaper has an active campaign to get more business women readers.

You can help yourself immensely if you will broaden your reading interests to include business magazines and newspapers. If you visualize their pages as dull and just something for economists and the like, you may be pleasantly surprised. Do take a look and see for yourself.

As you read and build your clipping file, you will find help, encouragement, and ideas for your future.

What About Your Responsibilities at Home?

In April 1972 Revised Order 4 marked an end to many of the questions usually asked of married women applying for jobs concerning their children, or the possibilities of pregnancy. This order requires companies with federal contracts of $50,000 or more, and fifty employees or more, to file affirmative plans for the equal employment of women. To comply with this order such a company must not, among other things, deny employment to women with young children, unless the same policy applies also to men. Nevertheless the dilemma of what to do with young children remains for many women.

You may not have any young children, but since more and more young mothers are going back to work, let's start with this difficult problem.

Once there were two subjects that could always turn a calm party into a raging battlefield: politics and religion. Now there seems to be a third: child care centers.

There are always pious critics who say, "Well, why do those women have children if they don't want to take care of them?" Many of these same people forget that the 1939 dollar was worth but 35 cents in 1971, and that costs are still rising. Many women, therefore, have no choice—they must leave their children to enter the labor market.

Society is constantly changing, but society usually does not welcome change. There are few improvements won without a struggle; so it is with day-care centers.

Working mothers have always had a part in our history. As Caroline Bird says in her book, *Born Female*:

In the colonies women enjoyed a scarcity value. The children they bore were badly needed and labor was so short that they worked alongside the men, even shooting down marauders when need be.

In colonial America, women became butchers, silversmiths, gunsmiths, upholsterers, jailkeepers, printers, apothecaries and doctors (or doctoresses, as they were called then). Women helped their men, and when they became widows they had no choice but to go on running the farm, store, mill, newspaper, and shipyard. Nantucket wives managed substantial enterprises for years while their husbands went on whaling trips.

In past generations most Americans lived on farms, or in small towns in what is now called the "extended family." Children, parents, and grandparents, possibly a maiden aunt, maybe a "hired girl," all lived in one household. No young mother had to bear the full responsibility for all the care of her children. Today two-thirds of American women live in cities far from their families. The mother often spends most of her time alone with her children in a small house or apartment. She must often bear the full responsibility for rearing the children, to the detriment of all concerned.

Women and their husbands might read the book *The Employed Mother in America* by Ivan Nye and Louis Hoffman. Contrary to earlier studies, which were made without controls, recent research indicates that children of working mothers are not different, in any significant way, from the children of women who stay at home. Similar evidence could be cited to show that husband-wife relationships do not suffer—and, in fact, may be strengthened.

How to Select a Child-Care Center

First of all, how do you find out your state's licensing requirements?

In the telephone directory, for example, you will find a listing like this:

Wisconsin State of —
Milwaukee
  Health and Social Services of —
    Family Services Division of —
      Licensing—Child Agencies & Institutions 224—4522
      State Office Building, Sixth Floor
      819 North Sixth Street

States vary in their licensing requirements. The Department of Health and Social Services, Division of Family Services, has a twenty-two page booklet describing the rules for licensing units of Day Care Centers for Children in Wisconsin.

Helen Alexander, child development administrator for eleven Day Care Services for Children, Inc., and a member of the Wisconsin Day Care Advisory Committee, has also offered some advice on the subject. Mrs. Alexander has a Bachelor of Philosophy degree from Cardinal Stritch College in Milwaukee, Wisconsin, and an M.S. degree from the University of Wisconsin, Milwaukee, in early childhood education and child development.

When asked what parents should look for in a good, licensed child-care center, Mrs. Alexander explained that the ones she was associated with more than met the state's minimal requirements. That is, they provide much more than just custodial care. All have trained teachers and paraprofessionals (apprentice teachers), both men and women. There are some men on the staff, since, as many times there is no father present in the home, it is important for the children to identify with a male image. There are also nurses, social workers, and nutritionists on the staff.

Mrs. Alexander added, saying what she would look for in a day care center, "One, I'd want to be sure the place conforms to all the safety regulations. Two, I'd want to know the qualifications of the staff. And above all, I'd want my child to be in a place where he could grow emotionally, socially, and intellectually.

"It is always a good idea for the parents to visit several places to observe the climate of the center and to see how the children react," she continued. "It is very important to prepare the child at home, too. Drive past the center on a weekend just to let him see it, then take the child to visit another day. If there is a father in the home, be sure to have him go, too. Many fathers bring the child to the center or pick him up after work."

In the past many centers, such as Head Start centers, were available solely for low-income families, but these have more recently been opened to families in the middle-income bracket. Costs to the family depend on income.

Mrs. Alexander spoke of the mothers who must work but have small babies at home. In 1968 Day Care Services for Children, Inc., initiated a project in which women in the inner city are trained and licensed to care for the younger children of mothers taking vocational training under Opportunities for the Future (OFF). The family-care mothers are trained, licensed, and paid by the state to meet the needs of the children in the house they will be in. The family-care mother may take care of as many as three babies in one home. This also means that the children in school have someone to watch over them until their mother gets home.

"This project benefits three groups," Mrs. Alexander said. "The children are the obvious ones to gain. But the family-care mothers have been able to leave welfare, and the children's mothers are learning jobs that will do the same for them."

The family-care mothers meet occasionally at the Day Care Services for Children, Inc., central office to discuss mutual problems. When a child has a physical or behavior problem the family-care mother cannot meet, she is told to inform the office so they can help her. One reason these family-care mothers are so successful is that they have empathy for mothers who must work. They've met most of the problems themselves—desertion by parents, growing up in poverty, abandonment by husbands, rearing problem children, and living on welfare.

Some other states have family-care mothers, too. To get such information, write to your state's Department of Health and Social Services, Division of Family Services.

For further information, Mrs. Alexander recommended the reading list suggested by the National Association for the Education of Young Children, Editorial and Publications Office, 104 East 25 Street, New York, N.Y. 10010.

Private Day-Care Centers

To meet the demands for day-care services for working middle-class mothers, private companies have entered the field. To quote from an article in *The New York Times* in spring of 1972:

The tending of preschool children is a new and booming industry for service and franchising companies. The entrepreneurs see an insistent demand by working mothers as well as those who want greater daytime freedom, for safe, professionally directed places where they can leave their children.

Unlike the Federally funded or nonprofit day-care centers for welfare or low-income mothers, these new day-care facilities are designed as business ventures.

If there were any doubts about the demands for day-care services at rates within reach of middle-income mothers, they were emphatically removed by the findings of a year-long survey, recently completed. . . .

The survey concluded that there are now more than 4 million American mothers with children under 6 who either have to work or choose to. Yet the survey found that there are licensed day-care facilities, in all categories, for only 700,000 children throughout the country.

James A. Leidich, the enthusiastic twenty-nine-year-old president of one such franchising company, sees great profit potential in day-care facilities.

"There's no doubt the social patterns in this country are changing rapidly," he said recently. "Mothers who have been trained in college for careers want to pursue them. There are hundreds of others who have to work to support themselves. They could not or would not qualify for welfare. A private day-care center is the only thing for them. The demand is certainly there, and so is potential return."

Mr. Leidich said he was well aware of the skepticism among many educators over the quality of profit-making centers, particularly those franchised nationally. "Certainly there will be plenty of protest over the idea of Kentucky fried children," he said. "But first they should find out whether we are helping the child, as well as the mother. We're operating with professional teachers, and we're offering a lot more than just a parking place."

Among such franchise companies are the three Learning Tree day-care centers operating in the Minneapolis-Saint Paul area, and the five centers in the Dayton, Ohio, area operated by Social Dynamics. This company has merged its day-care operations with those of a publicly owned corporation in Dallas, Texas, which operates eight centers there. Mary Moppets Day Care School, Inc., has forty-two centers in areas such as Grand Rapids, Michigan,

Albuquerque, New Mexico, Omaha, Nebraska, and Colorado Springs, Colorado.

Alphabetland Pre-School Centers, operating from Long Island, has seventeen day-care centers in New York, New Jersey, and Florida. Fees range from $17 a week in Phoenix to $50 a week in the New York City area, depending on how many hours and days a child spends at a center. Most of the profit-making centers operate for at least twelve hours during the day. Some arrange to pick up children after school and keep them until their mothers are finished working.

What About the Older Children?

The preschool child is not the only worry for the working mother. What about the child when he comes home from school or when he is free during the summer months? Many working mothers depend on relatives or in the summer, high school baby sitters to help out.

Day-care centers are principally for young children, but the YWCA in some cities offers an eight- to ten-week day camp for boys and girls seven to ten years whose mothers are employed, and Day Care Services for Children, Inc., offers an eight-week program of fun and learning for children ages six to twelve who need full day supervision.

Many mothers worry as much about teenagers in the summer months as they do about preschoolers. When the teens are too young to get a regular job, one solution is the volunteer job. The Volunteer Bureau of your United Community Services will take both boys and girls as young as fifteen for a variety of jobs that will give them valuable job training for the future. The youngsters work in hospitals, playgrounds, and in day-care centers. In many cases, these volunteer jobs give the young people guidance in their choice of careers in later life.

If it is possible, a good solution may be for the husbands and wives to arrange their work hours so that one parent is always at home.

For example, at the First Wisconsin National Bank, there is one shift from 10:00 P.M. to 6:00 A.M. three nights a week. Most of the women on that shift are young mothers. They prefer these hours because their husbands can baby-sit. It is interesting to talk to these young fathers and hear their reactions. Most of them enjoyed the experience. "I'm really getting to know my kids," was a frequent comment. Equally frequent is the mother's comment: "My husband can handle the children as well as or better than I can." It is gratifying to see couples share the responsibility of child rearing.

Bear in mind that most sociologists support the theory that it is the *quality* of the time a mother gives her children, not the *quantity*, that makes her a successful mother.

How Will You Manage the Work at Home, Especially If You Work Full Time?

A few years ago, at back-to-work clinics and in articles about women going back to work, all seemed to start with the premise that if the husband objected it wouldn't work. Said one woman, "My husband objected at first, but after he saw what a difference it made in our lives, how much better we could live on two incomes, he stopped objecting. We've been able to travel in every state in the union." Another said, "My husband objected too, at first. But then he said he noticed the improvement in my dinner table conversation since I went back to work. It made me wonder what I must have talked about before."

Now the problem is not so much husbands objecting to work outside the home but how a woman can still do all the work expected at home. This is difficult, if not impossible, if you have a full-time job.

Before you take a job, it is always wise to have a family consultation about who is going to help with what. Each family will have its own solutions, but many working mothers have said, "Teach the children to take on responsibility as early as possible. By the time they are teenagers they'll love you for it. We all know helpless kids who can't run appliances, fry an egg, or oil the lawn-mower."

All agree that it is best to be consistent in what is expected. "It only confuses the children if you're soft one day and act like a drill sergeant the next."

One mother said, "I have five children. I write down all the household chores I know they can do, put them in a box, and they can each take a chance on which slip they'll draw. They like the element of surprise, and that way they don't get tired of always doing the same thing."

Some working mothers weary of being the family chauffeur. One told me how she found a new form of transportation for her teens and near teens. She said, "Well, I just thought it was about time kids walked to where they want to go. I love to read history, so I told them what one pioneer wrote of the early days when her family settled near what is now Belvidere, Illinois, when all around was wilderness. The early settlers brought their tools from Scotland, and they not only built their own log cabins but were prepared to do other carpentry as well.

"This pioneer woman wrote: 'A man in Belvidere asked father to help him with some carpentry, so father walked eight miles there prepared to stay one night. He took my brother, George, then about nine years old, with him as it was necessary to send the child back with some much needed supplies for our family. It was a long, lonesome walk for the small boy, over a trackless country of wood and brush and not a habitation between our cabin and what is now Belvidere. George had never been far from home before, so father thoughtfully took his hatchet along and blazed a trail as they walked along so George could find his way home, which he did in safety for he was a brave son of a brave pioneer. As I think of it now, it was taking a great risk, as there might have been Indians lurking about or wild beasts.' "*

Continued my friend, "Can you imagine! My kids think I'm terrible if I don't drive them eight blocks! But evidently no one in that era ever thought little George couldn't do this. I said to my young ones, 'If that child could walk eight miles where there wasn't even a path through the woods, you can walk eight blocks.'

* From "The Argyle Settlement" by Daniel G. Harvey. Privately published in 1924.

To tell you the truth, I'm not sure it made too much impression on them, but then they discovered ecology, so now they're walking."

American women are thought to be surrounded by all kinds of mechanical help and to have very little to do in the home. Actually a recent survey indicates that women with young children work 99.6 hours per week!

From time to time in my personnel job, I have had foreign visitors, some from India, Japan, Korea, and other countries. A woman from the Labor Ministry in India on her first trip to the United States said to me, "I am astounded at how hard American women work! I cannot imagine how they manage to work in an office job and then do all they do at home without any help. At home, I have many servants to help me." A woman executive from Korea said, "I have three maids at home. How can American women do all this without help?" The business women from Japan had similar views.

A woman personnel director talked with me about cultural conditioning. "It does seem to make so much difference in men's attitudes about helping with housework. I think of my father whenever I hear men object to helping their working wives. All my forebears were Scots. It's probably no accident that one of the greatest essays ever written about the equality of women was that by famed Scottish economist, John Stuart Mill. And think of it—this was in 1869. He was way ahead of his time. And so was my father, I believe. He never looked down on anyone or any job. He was a secure man. It does seem as though it's the insecure people who always want to look down on other persons or jobs.

"When I was a child, father never expected mother to do all the housework as so many men do. He always provided a girl to help her. We were away in college in depression days. Father could no longer afford to pay help for mother, so he always helped her. He never acted put upon or apologetic about it. Never tried to disguise the fact he did this. He was a very strong leader in the community. Everyone looked up to him and admired him."

As a result, when this woman went into personnel work, she had little trouble working with people of all kinds because her father had taught her that everyone is important. And that people must be treated as individuals, not types

Another woman said, "We really need my income to support our family, but I'm so tired trying to do my job and all the housework, too, I can hardly keep going. The women's magazines have all those articles about 'How to Help Your Husband.' I've never seen anything in men's magazines about 'How to Help Your Wife.' "

She was surprised when I told her that *The Wall Street Journal* had published just such an article in 1970. It was called "Let George Do It. Women's Lib Movement Inspires More Couples to Strive for Equality. One Husband Irons Dresses, Others Baby-sit or Cook."

That this particular newspaper published such an unexpected article like this is not surprising. In fact, at a writers' conference the editor of a religious magazine told the writers that *The Wall Street Journal* has some of the best-written articles they could find anywhere, including many articles you might find helpful for your files. Some of its front page articles have included: "Year-Round Schools Win Increasing Support of Parents, Teachers"; "Learning to Learn. New Techniques Help Pupils Who Can't Grasp Fundamental Concepts"; "Vasectomies Increase as Concern over 'Pill,' Overpopulation Grows"; "New Tack on Cancer. Doctors Plan Trials of Less Drastic Cures for Tumors of Breast"; "Drugs in Suburbia. Children of Affluence, Bored and Disillusioned, Turn to Pot and Pills."

Naturally, the rest of the paper will give you an education that will be helpful to you in your return to the business world.

Where Can You Find Household Help?

Lack of household help is one of the greatest hindrances for women who want to pursue careers in the professions or advance to management posts.

No one is more aware of this than Elizabeth Duncan Koontz, director of the Women's Bureau, U.S. Department of Labor. The Women's Bureau has found in its studies that there is not only a great need for trained, expert household skills, but that many women, if they could, would choose to earn their living, or help their budgets by selling these skills where they are needed. But many have hesitated to head for housework because it has no status, low pay, and there is little legislation to protect such workers.

Two years ago Mrs. Koontz started to do something about this. She says, "If we are agreed that there is a great need for the services of workers skilled in home-related arts, and that the plight of those presently in household employment makes this an unattractive occupational choice, then we must accept the fact that the social and economic status of private household workers must be changed, the occupations must be reconstituted, and the industry restructured. Expert training programs, decent pay standards, dignity, and employers with the right attitudes—these are what it takes to make all this work."

That there is a great need to give the job more status is shown by this fact: in the *Dictionary of Occupational Titles* currently used in employment services, jobs are rated according to complexity of skills in relation to data, people, and things. The symbol used for the highest complexity is 0 and 8 is used for the least complex.

"Homemaker" is rated 878; that is, it is rated as the least complex of jobs, requiring the least skill. It is given the same rating as a parking lot attendant and rest room attendant. This rating is shocking to any woman who has ever attempted what is actually a highly complex job!

Three states have moved to give minimum wage coverage to private household workers. Wisconsin (July 1, 1970), Massachusetts (November 23, 1970), and New York (January 15, 1972).

The Women's Bureau has an excellent leaflet that gives a great deal of advice and suggestions. It is called "If Only I Could Get Some Household Help!" Single copies may be obtained by writing the Women's Bureau, U.S. Department of Labor, Washington, D.C. 20210.

Also, the National Committee on Household Employment, 1436 Connecticut Ave. N.W., Washington D.C. 20036, has materials on how to develop standards for household employment and pay, where there are existing training programs, and how to start organizing all this in a community.

Income Tax Deductions for Child Care and Other Dependents' Expense

In 1972, the government changed the tax rules for dependents. The new rules will benefit families with working mothers, women who are heads of households, fathers rearing children alone, many working couples, and individuals caring for dependent adults.

Be sure to check the new rules, as they can mean a substantial saving and are far more realistic than the old rule, which allowed only $900 as a maximum deduction for child care expense.

Chapter 4

How Much Does Appearance Count?

Your appearance and bearing carry an immediate message to the employment interviewer, and especially to the person responsible for hiring.

One personnel director said, "My eye instinctively takes in the applicant's appearance. I can't see her ability in that first glimpse, but I can see whether her clothes are appropriate, and her appearance attractive."

Being neat and clean is as important as the clothes you wear—clean skin, clean teeth, clean clothes, clean hair. Someone once said, "There are no really unattractive women—just *indifferent* women." Careless grooming will undermine all of your other efforts. There is something very negative and unappetizing about dank, dirty hair and big, dirty toes sticking out of sandals, for instance.

Fortunately for employers, the mature woman who comes back to work was reared in an era before organized sloppiness became almost the required uniform for many young people today.

Hints About What to Wear for a Job Interview

1. "Beware of all occasions requiring new clothes," said philosopher Henry David Thoreau.

More recently, Barbara Walters, female star of the NBC *Today* show, said in her book, *How to Talk with Practically Anybody About Practically Anything,* "A nervous making situation is no time for a new dress, even though that's what we usually think will help."

You will be much more at ease in something you've worn before. You won't have to wonder then about the fit or whether the dress wrinkles easily, among other things. As for new shoes—remember the time you wore new shoes on a vacation and wound up with aching feet? Well-fitting shoes are an absolute must for a business-woman. You can never feel smart if your feet hurt.

2. When you go in for an interview, you are like the woman who is preparing to make a speech. So a hint about how she selects clothes may help you: The best-dressed speaker is one whose audience is least concerned with, or distracted by, what she is wearing.

Simple, classic clothes are the best. "Shock treatment belongs in psychiatry," says famed designer Anne Klein, whose classic clothes have long been admired. Therefore, avoid the "drop dead" look. You can wear something flashy at a party for fun, but getting a job is no place for this tactic.

All of us have probably worn some adaptation of the Chanel suit. One of the really great designers, Mlle Chanel was still actively working on her next collection when she died, well into her eighties, in 1971. She helped generations of women with her philosophy about clothes. Among other things, she said, "Dress to please. Not to astonish." And, "The most important thing to remember about fashion is that it isn't always right to be always in fashion." She scorned that constant upsy-daisy bit about hemlines, and kept hers at about the same length when the winds of fashion change were blowing all around her. Her influence lives on. The comfortable Chanel suit has become almost a uniform for women of all ages.

Jewelry, if worn, should be simple, and without jangling or glitter.

Many Women Complain Because They Can't Find Suitable Clothes

There are those who feel that manufacturers and advertisers have done a disservice to the over-thirty-five market in overappealing to the more youthful figures and sizes.

Many women who really want to buy classic clothes just can't find them in sizes they could wear. They write pleading letters to stores, all with the same complaint: "When are designers and manufacturers going to start making clothes for mature women? When we're over forty, we don't want to dress like our daughters or granddaughters, but we do want simple classic fashions that are kind to our figures, in flattering colors, and at prices we can afford. We're not all size 10, 8, and under, as many stores seem to think!"

Equally frustrated are the older women, who can wear size 10 and under but can't find anything that doesn't look like a kicky Junior Miss.

Good News May Be on the Way

According to *Women's Wear Daily:*

Working women and their life styles are changing the scope of retailing simply by their presence in the nation's labor pool.

In a major study prepared by the Bureau of Advertising for presentation at the National Retail Merchants Association meeting in New York City, the bureau said, "the working woman has acquired distinct habits increasing her stature as a person and as a customer!"

The bureau suggests retailers adapt to the working woman by making it easier for her to shop, provide time-saving services, and appealing directly to her with ads and layouts she understands. For example, stores could limit the variety of departments where a woman buys dresses. The ads, the bureau says, could also show a "work background" since working women are relating more to that than other areas. . . . The study says 71 per cent of the working women say they have the job in mind when they shop for clothes.

A leading merchant at the same convention declared, "It would appear that retailers know little about working women—who they are, what they need, where they shop, and how to do business with them."

He added, "In recent years, some retailers have played hide-and-seek games with shoppers, daring them to find goods in a freaky, boutiquey, merry-go-round."

What You Can Do to Get Better Clothes

Women seem more confident of their fashion sense now. They refuse to be dictated to. Said many, "I'd *had it* with the 'new look' when I was a girl. So when they trotted out the 'midi,' I said 'nothing doing—I won't buy it.' "

Today's women want things simpler—useful but not fussy. They don't want bulky skirts that get in their way when they climb in and out of cars whose designs gets smaller and smaller each year. They want easy care, multi-occasion clothes. And since almost all offices are air-conditioned, the working woman can now have more clothes that are for all seasons.

1. It helps to learn how to sew, even if you don't have time to make all your clothes. Teen-age daughters are often helpful. Sewing is said to be the number-one hobby among teenagers, and 90 percent of all teen girls know how to sew. The present estimate of home sewers in the United States is between 42 and 45 million.

When you know how to sew, you get into the habit of looking inside a ready-made garment to see how wide the seams are, the depth of the hem, the stitching, and such other details as the fit at the shoulders. A poor fit there can spoil the looks of any garment. Check, too, to see if there are holes to mark the darts, because if there are, nobody can alter those darts to change the fit.

Sewing is not only a creative art, but, after coping with office problems all day, is relaxing for many. There is something very gratifying about being able to follow dress pattern instructions and have the garment turn out the way it is supposed to look. And, as a government official in the state employment service told me, "Any woman who can read dress pattern instructions should have no trouble getting a good paying job in a factory where you read similar types of instructions to put things together."

There was a time when I made all my clothes, even suits, hardest of all garments to make. This sewing knowledge made me a better buyer, since I became knowledgeable about fabrics and began to appreciate good workmanship. Good tailoring costs money, but well-made classics last a long time, and can be the backbone of your wardrobe.

Many smart women collect accessories to vary the classics. Here's where your filing system can help. Clip the articles about various ways to wear scarves, for instance, or pictures of interesting belts. Study the expensive shop windows to see how they have harmonized units of clothing with accessories.

2. Put your faith in a reliable saleswoman and try to have the same person help you each time you're in the store. If she appreciates your interest, she'll give you good advice and help build your fashion sense and self-confidence.

3. Complain. If you can't find the kind of understated, easy-care garments in your size, complain to the stores. Write to the consumer education writers whose columns so many newspapers and magazines publish. One of these columnists reported that she received hundreds of letters from women complaining about poor workmanship and lack of suitable sizes. She, in turn, forwarded these complaints to the manufacturers. So never feel there is nothing you can do. Speak up! Multiple voices generate *action*!

Where to Find Help in Taking Care of Clothes

The Federal Trade Commission has had many complaints about labels on clothing about washing, dry cleaning, and other care. In your file you should keep such labels, because, with so many man-made fibers now, one really needs these guides so the garment won't be ruined with the wrong kind of care.

The Federal Trade Commission has asked manufacturers to put more detailed labels on clothing. These labels must be on most clothes that are shipped after July 3, 1972.

To help you with your clothing care problems, you can write to National Institute of Drycleaning, Inc., 909 Burlington Avenue Silver Spring, Md. 20910. The Institute has many leaflets to guide you in clothing purchase and care.

Also write to American Institute of Laundering, Joliet, Ill. 60434. The Institute has booklets, not only about clothes but other household items as well.

A working woman doesn't need many clothes if she will take good care of the ones she has. Rotating your clothes makes them last much longer: wool has to rest, as does leather.

What About Dress Regulations in Offices Today?

There was a time when most offices had strict dress regulations, but most employers today allow anything in good taste.

1. What about pants suits? They no longer cause gasps of "What next?" in most offices. They are good-looking, unlike the casual attire of slacks and shirts, which don't seem to fit into many offices. As the late Fred Allen once said, "I've never seen much slack in slacks." Few women look like movie actresses in them. Actually, it's only been in comparatively recent years that pants have been strictly male attire—Turkish, Chinese, and Eskimo women have worn them for centuries—and men were once comfortable in togas and tunics.

2. What about skirt lengths? There has been much confusion recently because of the controversy over lengths. But when it comes to the "mini," the "maxi," or knee-length skirts, choose the one you feel most comfortable in and that seems to fit your particular physical characteristics best. There just isn't any one ideal length any more. Women have freedom to use their own discretion.

3. What about hot pants? That's a different story. One executive groaned. "I dread the summer. The wrong people always wear those things." Many offices will not allow them. After all, going to work is not like going to a beach party. Being well-dressed means being dressed *appropriately.*

Career Apparel

Some employers, either tired of trying to monitor dress, or confused by the proliferation of styles, have recently turned to designers to come up with uniforms that will be neat, comfortable, and acceptable to employees. However, they no longer call them "uniforms," but "career apparel."

"Why did you start using uniforms?" someone asked the executive of a large company.

"I'll tell you if you won't use my name," he replied cautiously. "It all boils down to the way people look on the job. I went around to all our offices a few years ago, and I couldn't believe what I saw.

"Dozens of customer service clerks were dressed in everything from five-dollar housedresses to cocktail party finery with low necklines. It was unbelievable!"

The "uniforms" followed. The employees didn't like them at first. The executive explained, "We tried the Tom Sawyer approach. We let a few people who liked the idea go ahead and get official clothes while the rest stayed in civvies. The others saw what they were missing, and pretty soon I started getting petitions demanding uniforms for everybody."

Do all women like them? The National Association of Bank Women made a survey of representative firms in various sections of the country. There was no agreement on this subject. Some banks reported that at first the tellers and others who wore the uniforms were enthusiastic but became bored with the sameness. Others felt career apparel took away a person's individuality.

In addition to having career apparel, some firms—especially banks, utilities, and insurance companies—have fashion shows during the noon hour in their cafeterias in an effort to keep the dress tone above average. Many who tried this report that the cafeterias are always packed on the days of the fashion shows.

Good Health

Good health is not only significant in maintaining a favorable appearance, but it can be a deciding factor in getting the job to begin with. A pre-employment physical examination for all new employees is standard practice in many companies.

Many applicants are approved without reservation. Others are approved with qualifications because of conditions that are correctable, such as impaired vision, poor teeth, or hearing loss

1. Impaired vision. It is important to have the right glasses before you try to take employment tests.

2. Poor teeth. Dental problems not only affect your looks, but also interfere with proper nutrition. Poorly fitted dentures can affect the line of the mouth and the jaws and may make eating so difficult that nutrition suffers.

3. Hearing loss. It is said that 20 million people in this country,

ranging in age from young children to senior citizens, are afflicted with some degree of hearing loss. I have seen women hold themselves back in jobs because they don't want to admit they have a hearing loss.

The National Bureau of Standards has published a new booklet called "Facts About Hearing and Hearing Aids." It costs 60 cents. Write to the Consumer Product Information Distribution Center, Washington, D.C. 20407. The booklet gives advice on where and to whom to go for different types of medical analysis of hearing loss. The various kinds of specialists, both medical and hearing aid device experts, as well as speech and hearing centers and health clinics, are listed. The booklet also cites sources of financial assistance for those on limited budgets.

Nutrition, Exercise, and Overweight

You may be in better physical shape than your children! When Bonnie Prudden, famed physical fitness teacher, gave a talk to adults, she asked them, "How many of you walked to school?" and "How many of you ran around during recess?" Many said they had. "How many of you walked—no, you ran home for lunch because there wasn't much time?" If you've kept up some sort of exercise on a regular basis, you may be ahead of your school-age children, who spend so much time at a desk and walk very little.

However, there are millions of us who have to keep fighting the flab battle. If you are greatly overweight, you may be rejected in a pre-employment physical. Your obesity may also cause high blood pressure and other ailments. And don't forget that it is so much easier to find clothes if one is not too fat. What an uncomfortable feeling it is when those seams are tight! J. M. Barrie once remarked, "She seemed not so much dressed as upholstered."

A sane, sensible diet is the best answer to your weight problem. As all of you know, no one should go on a diet without consulting a physician. In recent years, with the approval of their doctors, thousands of men and women have taken off weight sensibly through the various group reducing methods. I know this method works, because I've tried it myself. It was a re-education of eating habits approved by my doctor. It was also fun, and I was never hungry.

Proper nutrition is very important. As an official in the Department of Agriculture said, "Although we live in the most affluent society on earth, about forty-five percent of the people in the United States suffer mostly minor, but in some cases severe, malnutrition. Millions eat what they want to eat. Not what they should."

You won't lack for reading matter in magazines about nutrition. In addition you can get many sound booklets on this subject from the National Dairy Council. This is a nonprofit research and educational organization of the dairy industry. Dairy Council nutrition education materials are designed and developed to meet the varied needs of professional, educational, and consumer groups and to provide authentic information and teaching aids about dairy foods and their contribution to nutritional well-being.

To get the catalogue describing its publications, write to National Dairy Council, 111 North Canal Street, Chicago, Ill. 60606. Listed in this catalogue are the locations of Dairy Council offices throughout the United States. If you live in one of these Dairy Council areas, some of the materials are free. Some are printed in Spanish, such as "Guide to Good Eating" and "Easy Meals That Please."

Your Hair and Figure

Many personnel experts agree that the two most out-of-date conditions about a woman when she goes back to work are her figure and her hair.

Keep hair styles soft and natural. Straggly hair always seems to add years to a mature woman's looks. A good haircut is one of the best investments she can make.

Working women are always looking for ways to save time. A wig can be a real life saver and a time saver as well. A wig gives the hair a chance to rest, too, since the wearer doesn't have to bleach, spray, or do whatever else is in fashion to her own hair.

It is estimated that between 10 and 15 million women wear wigs on occasion, and many own more than one.

Wigs are considered by the Federal Trade Commission to fall under the Flammable Fabrics Act because they are worn, just as a scarf is worn, on the person. As yet, only one man-made fiber can be called "flame resistant," and that's modacrylic. Some wigs are highly flammable, and the FTC hunts them down as fast as possible. Check labels to see whether modacrylic has been used, or if a flame-resistant treatment has been applied that would meet current standards.

Wigs can put some fun in your life. The washable, synthetic ones are no harder to wash than your nylons, but be sure to follow instructions.

Your Cosmetics

Chanel once said, "Nature gives you your face at twenty, life models your face at thirty, but it's up to you to deserve your face at fifty."

The natural look seems to be the favored one now, but for mature women it takes a little doing to achieve the natural look. When we're over eighteen we can't expect just to scrub our faces and meet the world with confidence. We must enhance what we have to start with.

A Hollywood makeup man and photographer said, "My best advice for the woman who isn't sure of the makeup she needs is to visit the cosmetics department of a large department store. All the girls who work there are trained, and they know what they're talking about. It's the best free information a woman can get anywhere."

Many women look unnecessarily drab because they haven't changed their makeup for twenty-five years. Soft, subtle makeup creams in a shade close to your own can hide minor defects, and a "blusher" can add a sparkling highlight when properly applied to the cheeks. If you have never used eye makeup, purchase only a brand and type that you will feel comfortable with. That means generally a subdued eye shadow, perhaps, or eye liner plus mascara in the shade closest to the natural one of your own eyebrows. Practice applying it at home, both to accustom yourself to your new look and to become used to applying it quickly and easily.

Barbara Walters, whose book I mentioned previously, has some good advice about makeup. Since she is seen five days a week in millions of homes, you can see for yourself what a good example she is, both in her dress and in her makeup.

Makeup for Darker Skins

Long, long overdue in stores has been makeup for darker skin. This makeup has been regularly available in black communities, such as Harlem, but not until recently obtainable across the country. There are said to be at least five companies in the nation that have responded to this growing market by manufacturing aids specifically for black skins.

I talked with a young woman who developed her cosmetic line because she had such a hard time finding the right cosmetics when she was an actress. She said her products now are in more than a hundred stores. As she explained, "Stock makeup for whites is not right for black women. It makes their eyes recede, their faces ashen, and it lights up their lips like neon signs."

If you cannot find the kind of makeup appropriate for your own coloring, ask about it. Write a letter to the store president, or write to your favorite consumer-education columnist.

Three-fourths of the world's population is composed of races with dark skins, and yet it is not easy to find books that suggest the colors and cosmetics that will enhance their beauty. A few years ago I found such a book, called *How to Wear Colors with Emphasis on Dark Skins*, by Charleszine Wood Spears. It was designed as a supplementary text for high school and college courses in costume design. The author said she wrote it because, at that time, few if any high schools or universities offered courses that give specific information regarding colors in relation to the different types of dark skins.

Parts of the book are now dated, such as references to afternoon dresses, which are not worn any more, or to hats, which hardly anyone bothers with. But the book does have some very useful and detailed information about the various types of dark skins and colors for them.

Concern About Cosmetics

Have you ever thought how odd it is that we don't know what is in the cosmetics we use? The Food and Drug Administration insists that our food be labeled. The FDA and the American Medical Association have been probing for years to try to find out the exact ingredients in cosmetics. No law as yet requires manufacturers to list the contents on the jars and bottles we buy.

Rep. Leonor Sullivan (D.-Mo.) has frequently introduced legislation requiring labeling. A similar bill introduced by Rep. Frank E. Evans (D.-Colo.) picked up thirty-eight co-sponsors in early 1972. About sixty thousand Americans have serious cosmetic reactions every year. If you should be one of them, *complain!* Write to your congressman or congresswoman and ask them to support the legislation requiring labeling.

Most women like to give nature a helping hand by using cosmetics. But still we'd like to know what we're putting on our faces, wouldn't we?

Your Posture and Voice

Your posture, your voice, the way you wear your clothes—these can do so much for your confidence. The slouchers, slumpers, and grunters look and sound defeated before they even get into an interview.

In my youth I worked for a woman who was a model to all of us in many ways. She had a magnificent carriage. When she walked into a room everything about her suggested zest and good spirits. She had a springy step, held her head high, and talked with enthusiasm. She would have looked gracious in anything, but you were never as aware of her clothes as you were of her. She was always impeccably groomed, so you were never distracted by noting rundown heels, a soiled collar, or a too-long slip. She radiated an air of excitement as though she were anticipating that today might be a very meaningful day.

I count myself fortunate in having worked for her, because women need role models in the business world. If every applicant could walk in for an interview with the zest, posture, and confidence that this woman, the late Coyla F. Bell, had, she wouldn't have too much trouble finding a job.

Your voice can be important, too. Speech expert Dorothy Sarnoff says, deploringly, "Eight out of ten women talk with a nasal voice, which is the sound of the nag, the depressed, the frustrated, the weary. The lower the voice, the more persuasive." In her book, *Speech Can Change Your Life*, Miss Sarnoff describes more than two hundred ways to improve your total image and avoid negative impressions that derive from careless and sloppy speech habits. She sums up proper speech and lively conversation in these words: "Really the name of the game is warm communication."

And that is exactly what you want to do, not only with your voice, but also with your appearance, your reflection of good health and your positive zest for living.

Chapter 5

Where to Find Job Leads

"I couldn't go back to the state employment service," said one woman who was having difficulty returning to the job market. "Why, I haven't been in that office since I first got a work permit at the age of seventeen."

It is unbelievable how little many people know about the state employment service in their area and the many free services it can render. Today there are over two thousand such offices in the United States. If you do not know where the nearest one is located, try asking at your post office.

Most state employment services provide special services for the following groups, among others:

1. Young people, particularly those who are just starting to enter the job market and have little or no knowledge of where to turn.

2. Disadvantaged adults. An important aspect of the work of the state office is to upgrade the employability of adults, no matter what their problems. In large cities the state employment service has an "outreach" program, which goes into the slums with special programs to help the people there.

3. Individuals with mental or physical disabilities that constitute vocational handicaps are given special consideration.

4. Veterans. Each local office has a veterans' employment representative who is informed about veterans' rights and benefits and seeks to develop jobs for veterans. Since many women are veterans

of the various branches of the service, don't overlook this source of job leads and training.

5. Professional people. The state employment service has both the authority and the experience in placing professional people, including recent college graduates.

6. Older workers. Middle-aged and older workers are assisted in making realistic job choices and overcoming problems related to getting and holding jobs.

In big cities these special services are not always in the same location. In the telephone directory in Wisconsin, for instance, look under name of state, city, then "Industry, Labor and Human Relations, Dept. of." Under that will be the locations of the various services. The telephone listing varies in different states.

State employment services in big cities usually have an ad in the Yellow Pages of the telephone book, in the employment agency section. Here will be listed the services and the location of each.

If there is no state employment service near you, write to your capital city, state employment service, to ask whether they have a traveling representative and when such a representative will be in the town nearest you. These representatives travel throughout the state and can be consulted when they are in various small towns.

State Employment Service Aids to
Spanish-Speaking People

For the first time the Bureau of the Census has compiled statistics for persons of Spanish origin in the United States. They number about 5 percent of the population. Of this, grown women account for 3.5 percent of the total female labor force. Spanish was reported as the mother tongue of 6.7 million persons and as the current language of 4.6 million persons, making Spanish the second most commonly spoken language in the United States.

Therefore, in the big cities or in areas where large numbers of Spanish-speaking persons reside, there are interviewers and counselors who speak Spanish in the state employment service.

The public employment service began in 1834, in New York

City where it served purely as a labor exchange. Ohio, California, and Oregon soon established the same kind of exchange. Gradually other states followed suit, and in the 1930s the service was greatly expanded. Yet the past few years have seen more changes in the philosophy of the employment service than have occurred in the more than 130 years that preceded.

As you can see, the state employment service:

1. Helps people become successfully employed by giving them:
   a. Job information
   b. Employment counseling
   c. Referral to job training
   d. Job placement
2. Helps employers meet their manpower needs.
3. Helps communities develop their manpower resources.

The state employment service is now, and will increasingly become, a far different operation from the old employment service in which an interviewer only matched a worker and a job. The new employment service now helps develop workers by helping people acquire marketable skills.

Your Visit to the State Employment Service

It is best to apply in person. You cannot get very much help for any job over the phone, but you can learn something from every interview you have. Every step you take will help you take another.

Be sure to take your résumé with you so you will have all your facts at hand, your glasses, social security number if you have one, proof of military service, if applicable. If you are a veteran, don't forget this on your records. This is especially important for civil service examinations.

After you fill out an application, the employment service interviewer will check your qualifications and experience against job orders on file. If there are jobs available for which you are qualified, the interviewer will give you a direct referral to the employer on a little slip, which you will present at the personnel department in the firm where the job is. If you do not qualify for jobs currently on file, your application will be filed and compared with future job orders in the occupation you've listed. You will be notified if an opening occurs.

Many women returning to work after a lapse of some years either don't know what they can do with today's jobs or else feel unsure of their skills. Some have an unrealistic idea of office jobs today. It can be of great assistance to make an appointment for an interview with a counselor.

What the Counselor Can Do For You

1. The counselor is a skilled, experienced, professional worker, with a broad knowledge of the kinds of work available.

2. The counselor will need to know about your abilities, training, interests, and work experience.

3. The counselor will help you assess your strong points and your weak ones.

4. To find out more about your general abilities, the counselor may suggest that you take the general aptitude battery of tests, developed to cover nine basic abilities related to sixty-two fields of work. These take about two and a half hours. If the counselor doesn't suggest the tests, I urge you to ask for them. They will help you overcome your fear of taking tests in private firms, and they may unearth abilities you never realized you had. (In a later chapter, you will learn how to prepare yourself for such tests.)

The counselor will make an appointment for you to take the tests, which may be given in a different location. But here is where some women give up. They've worked up enough steam to go to the state employment service. They find they'll have to come back if they want to see a counselor, and then, when they find out they should take some tests, in perhaps a different location, at a later date, some think, "What's the use?" Please don't give up so soon! Jobs are not that easy to get when you've been away from the job market. Try to remember that in recent years office jobs have changed a great deal. There is more specialization; more skills are needed; people require more occupational information than they did even a few years ago.

5. After seeing the tests, the counselor will try to help you work

out a job plan. Possibly you may need more basic education. There are many intelligent women who never finished high school, especially those of school age during the Depression years. The counselor can refer you to the school where you may take general educational development courses, upon completion of which you'll get a certificate that is the equivalent of a high school diploma. In some areas, now, these tests are given in Spanish.

I've met many working women who have taken the GED courses. One said, "It always bothered me because I was the only one in the family who didn't have at least a high school diploma. My children all have college degrees, so it was the proudest day of my life when I got that GED certificate. Now I think I'll go on to take some college courses." This woman had never gone beyond eighth grade, but she was able to finish the GED courses in a year and a half.

Maybe you have a high school diploma, but very little clerical training. If you feel that you don't have the money to get more education, the counselor can tell you whether you qualify for free courses under the Manpower Development Training Act or the Work Incentive Training program, or other federally aided training programs.

6. The state employment service works with all the community services, too, which often assists people to become more employable, or helps with family problems.

For example, I interviewed many women who had just come to the United States. Many of them had good office skills, but had great difficulty with English. The counselor might refer such women to the International Institute, which helps foreigners adjust to living in the United States and provides informal English classes to prepare them for more formal English classes in the regular schools.

I recall one Cuban woman, a widow with five children and an aged mother to support. She had had excellent training in a Cuban firm some years ago, but she needed further training in English to undertake the telephone part of a good job in the international banking division of a large firm. The fact that she could write and speak Spanish fluently was a definite asset to her there. The International Institute helped her get the further training she needed in American English.

Most foreigners naturally feel more comfortable in their native tongue, but for job purposes, it would help a great deal if they would try to speak English at home until they become more fluent.

7. Counselors improve personal traits. The counselor may talk with you about such things as your appearance, grooming, speech, manner, and some of the qualities employers look for. They offer these suggestions in an effort to help you, so try not to take offense if they make some constructive suggestions. The counselors know both the employers and what is expected in these matters, so it is better to let them tell you some of these things, if needed, than to find out the hard way yourself.

8. Counselors provide factual information. After your tests, if your counselor feels you are ready to try for some jobs without further training, he can give you facts about occupations, industries, and employment trends. He will help you learn about occupations by answering such questions as:

    a. What are the principal duties in this kind of work?

    b. What are the employment trends and chances of advancement?

    c. What are the requirements as to education, training, and experience?

    d. What are the wages or salary ranges, hours, and conditions of work for this type of job? Naturally these will vary some, depending on the specific job and type of business.

    e. Where can a return-to-work-housewife fit in?

It is a good idea, for future reference, to jot down the name of the interviewer you talk with and also the name of the counselor.

Keep a Notebook

It is a good idea, too, to have a job-hunting notebook, in which you can make notes immediately after you come home from an interview. Having a notebook will give you a feeling of accomplishment.

Looking for a job is like a detective looking for clues. One thing leads to another, and sometimes, when you least expect it, a lead will turn up. It may turn up right in your own home, since the state employment services in some big cities use spot announcements on television. They sometimes call this "Job Line" or "Job Opportunity." I know that people watch the state employment service job announcements because I found a number of good applicants through this source. One woman did so well in her job that she later started her own business!

There is no one perfect way to find a job. There are advantages and disadvantages to each method. Yet you will learn something from each method you try.

Employment Agencies

If you live in a big city, you can learn a good deal about private employment agencies by studying their ads in the Yellow Pages. In New York City about twenty-four pages in the classified directory are required to list all the agencies.

Here are some things to remember:

1. Commercial agencies need to be licensed by your state.

2. Some agencies are highly specialized: some handle only college graduates, some specialize in certain kinds of jobs.

3. Some advertise "Free to applicants. No fees. All paid by employers." Others say, "Free and Fee jobs." Still others say "Fees Negotiable", i.e., the employer may pay it after seeing the applicant's qualifications and providing a trial period on the job.

4. Employers are most likely to pay the fees for hard-to-find applicants. Unless you have a readily marketable and up-to-date office skill, it is not too likely the employer will pay the fee.

5. It is advisable to register with a private employment agency. There is never any charge unless they find a job for you, at which time you will be asked to sign a contract if the employer doesn't pay the fee. Be sure to study the contract carefully so you will know its terms and charges.

A good employment agency can save you time in looking for a job, and its counselors can give you an evaluation of yourself and your job skills. They know what the state of the job market is and what your chances might be in it. They may suggest what further training you will need to meet the job requirements.

How do you find the best employment agencies? The best thing to do is to ask your friends and business acquaintances, if you live in or near a city. Indeed, word of mouth is a good way to find out about job openings themselves, especially in very small towns. Even in big cities, though, some of the news about job openings travels on the grapevine.

Try to Get Leads Through Friends and Business Acquaintances

Friends should not be expected to get a job for you, but they may be able to provide an introduction to people they know in business. Before you ask anyone to do this, it is wise to have "done your homework." I realize that many women are faced with the necessity of getting a job at once because death, divorce, or desertion plunges them into the working world.

Perhaps someone in your own family knows about a job opening in his office. Although there was a time when many offices had a rule that they would not employ close relatives, this is no longer true in most places. Many employers still say, though, that they do not want to hire any close relatives of top managers. In any event, your family members will know the rules of the firm and be guided accordingly.

The all-important thing is to get that interview in *person*—not over the phone or by mail.

Sending out letters of application and résumés is fine for recent high school and college graduates and for established business people, but, for someone who has been out of the work force for some time, this is not the best way to find a job.

Too many interviewers are likely to look at these letters and résumés, see that you haven't worked for some time, are forty-five, and show no degree of professional training. You may look really rusty on paper. Mature women vary so much in what they can do, and how they look and feel after they are thirty-five.

Just Walk In and Apply

If you don't know anyone who can introduce you, it's better just to walk in and apply, because you may arrive on the very day when there is a need for a person like you.

For example, I had just filled a job in the international banking division of a large firm where I had been asked for a fast and accurate typist in a beginning job. I sent in a recent high school graduate who scored very high in these matters. After two days, the manager called to say, "Please, you'll have to move Miss Jones out of our division. She can type fast all right, but she has absolutely no knowledge of foreign geography and doesn't know how to spell any European names."

That same morning a woman in her early forties applied. She was the kind of applicant who delights any personnel director: full of zest, articulate, and well educated. True, she had not worked recently except for a dab of typing here and there, because her husband had been a career army man. They had lived all over the world. A big plus was that she knew some foreign languages and could easily spell foreign names. Her enthusiasm about the job and eagerness to take the training courses offered delighted me. Moreover, she was willing to take the beginning job.

Unlike the high school girl who was just marking time until she got married, this woman had a husband who had just retired, and they both wanted to settle in one place. The fortyish woman preferred a job where she could advance. Because she was willing to study, a short time later she moved into the supervisory area.

Read the Want Ads in the Sunday Papers

Sunday is the best day for most firms to do their advertising. You can learn a good deal about the kinds of jobs most frequently open in offices, as well as the salary ranges, benefits, hours, and qualifications needed.

Start clipping these ads for future reference. You will see that some jobs, such as key punch operators, offer work in shift hours. And you can learn where some of the part-time jobs are.

Ads Should Be Desegregated

It is now illegal for want ads to express a preference for persons according to sex or age.

A few newspapers have desegregated them and now list all jobs under Help Wanted—Male/Female. Other newspapers get around the legal requirements by inserting a notice which may read something like this:

Looking for work? The headings of our "Help Wanted" and "Employment Agency" ads are used merely for the convenience of our readers, to let them know which jobs have historically been more attractive to persons of one sex than the other. The placement of an advertisement under a heading is not in itself an expression of a preference, limitation, specification, or discrimination based on sex. Employers who advertise here will consider any legally qualified applicant for a job without discrimination as to age or sex.

As of May 1971 the Civil Service Commission ruled that "men only" and "women only" requirements must be removed from most federal jobs. Federal agencies that are under civil service regulations will be allowed to choose employees by sex in only two areas —where jobs require employees to sleep in common quarters, or in certain institutional jobs, such as a matron in a women's prison.

When the telephone was new in the 1870s, all the operators were men. And when a certain firm hired the first woman about sixty-five years ago, they put a screen around her desk so that no customer would see and possibly take offense at the idea of a woman, instead of a man, typist in the firm.

It would seem that there are still employers who persist in thinking that some jobs are just for men and some are just for women. They sound like the descendants of those who put the barriers up and the screen around the woman sixty-five years ago.

The segregated want ads discriminate against both men and women. There are men who want stewards jobs on airplanes, or who want to be nurses or secretaries. Listing most of the management jobs under Help Wanted—Male only helps to perpetuate prejudice against women.

Study the Classified Section of the Telephone Directory

If you have had experience in a certain kind of job, check the index for the classification it is listed under and contact the companies within that listing.

The business office of many telephone companies have copies of directories from all over the United States. If you're moving to another state, it might pay you to study the Yellow Pages for possible job leads before you move.

Former Employers

If you had a good job record with a former employer, it always pays to try there.

Open an Account in a Bank— And You May Find a Job Lead!

There is more in a bank than money—possibly a good job lead. But you say, "I used to work in an interior decorator's office as a secretary. What would I do in a bank?"

I have located applicants for an interior decorator who needed a secretary, for an advertising agency, for industrial executives, for country club offices, and almost any business you might name. Customers have a way of calling their bank to ask if the bank can help them find office employees. It is not always possible to do this, but most banks are delighted to help a good customer if they can.

Then, too, you may be like Mrs. Pierce, who had just moved to a new city. When she opened a checking account, the officer asked her how she liked the city. Mrs. Pierce said, "I'd like it better if I had a job. I miss my work." Said the officer, "Why don't you go to see our personnel department?" and he told her where to go.

Moreover, bankers know about new firms locating in their city and sometimes may know of job leads there. Sometimes the new firm will ask a local bank to help them find job applicants even before they make the move.

Read the Newspaper Business Pages and
Real Estate Section of the Sunday Paper

For those of you living in small towns and suburbs, you may find that jobs are moving to your doorstep, because more firms are moving out of big urban centers.

Some small towns view these moves as a mixed blessing. For example, one very small town in the Midwest wasn't entirely happy when a manufacturing firm wished to build a plant in the town. It would mean giving up two hundred acres of good farm land. On the other hand, the plant would provide hundreds of new jobs, including some in the office, and the nearby farmers could sell their soy beans to the plant.

In 1940, 27 million or two out of every ten Americans lived in the suburbs. That was 19 million fewer than the cities. Now 76 million or almost four out of ten Americans live in the suburbs. This is 12 million more than the cities that spawned them.

In New York the population remains about evenly divided between urban and suburban. But in some cases the suburbs already are two, three, or four times as big as the inner cities they surround.

In 1940, most of the people who lived in the suburbs did not work there. Now as many as 60 percent of those who live in the suburbs also work there.

More and more you read, "XYZ company is building a 300-acre industrial park in what was formerly a quiet residential suburb." Or "Shopping center covering 135 acres will build near Quiettown." Or, "First high rise office building" in another bedroom surburb.

How do people feel when a shopping center covering 135 acres plants itself in a quiet suburb? Well, many women like it. A frequently heard comment is, "We like being able to work near home," or "It's great to be able to walk to work."

In some cities, smaller businesses are following the big ones to the suburbs. This is a migration of small, independent firms engaged in specialized enterprises. Many have small offices with only a few persons on the staff.

Many city workers like the move to the suburbs because they are tired of spending long hours commuting. Yet not everyone is happy about working in the suburbs or in small towns. Some firms have found it is harder to get younger workers, but that is a plus for the housewives who want to go back to work.

It pays, therefore, to read the real estate section of the Sunday newspapers. Here you'll often find articles about firms building new plants and offices for their moves to suburbs and small towns.

White-Collar Jobs Continue to Grow in Big Cities

In spite of all these moves away from urban centers, a nationwide study of office space made in 1971 by the Massachusetts Institute of Technology noted that from about 1 billion gross square feet in 1930, the nation's office space grew to about 2 billion in 1960 and 3 billion by 1970. The report states, "Barring a national disaster, there is no reason to expect a major or early downturn in this growth."

This growth continues to center in major metropolitan areas of at least one million people.

One-sixth of the nation's office space is in metropolitan New York. This area includes thirteen thousand square miles in three states. One third of the top five hundred industrial corporations have their headquarters there. Other metropolitan centers may be growing at a faster rate, but as of now few planners expect New York to lose its hold on the biggest single chunk of the white-collar job market.

Nonprofit Agencies to Contact

Urban League

Founded in 1910, the Urban League has done an outstanding job in helping blacks and other minority groups find jobs. It is a referral, community coordinating and social service agency. It provides vocational guidance and counseling to steer blacks and other minority groups into jobs, and it works with industry and labor groups to encourage the hiring of blacks and other minorities.

I've worked with the Urban League and know how untiring its efforts are to help the people who come for guidance. Equally important have been its ceaseless efforts to make employers aware of the talent going to waste if they do not make hiring minority workers part of their personnel program.

The Urban League has centers in ninety-eight major cities. To find out if there is a center in your city, write National Urban League, 55 East 52nd Street, New York, N.Y. 10022.

Jewish Occupational Council

Sometimes religious groups sponsor agencies that may range from job counseling to job placement. To find out about services sponsored by Jewish organizations write to the Jewish Occupational Council, 150 Fifth Avenue, New York, N.Y. 10010.

Clergymen

I talked with my minister about the help one might expect from a minister, priest, or rabbi. He said most modern clergymen could advise a parishioner where to go for job leads, such as the state employment service, and also tell whether the church or synogogue has any job referral service. He said, too, that sometimes clergymen hear about jobs in the course of their work.

You May Get a Lead Through a Tour

Because offices have changed so much in recent years, and because many women fear they may be out of step with the times, it would help you to get the feel of today's climate and place if you can take a tour of business firms. Many clubs arrange to do this. Or you may join a tour for your Cub Scout or Girl Scout troop. Or your child's teacher may have a class tour and would like some mothers to go along to keep order.

Another way to arrange a tour is through the convention and visitors bureau in your city. It can tell you which firms have tours and what person to call.

Checklist for Arranging Tours

1. Person to call
2. What he will want to know about your group:
   a. Why you are interested
   b. Number and age range (if children are coming) of those planning to attend
   c. Name, address, and phone number of person in charge of group
   d. Choice of dates

What You'll Want to Know

1. How much advance notice is needed
2. Time of tour and place to meet
3. How long the tour will be and how to get there
4. If questions may be asked during the tour
5. If parking space is available, and how much it is

Plans to Make for Your Group

Be sure everyone knows how to get there, where the tour will meet in the building, and at what time. Tell people about parking facilities and how long the tour will take.

Get confirmation in writing from the person in charge of tours at the firm.

Firms always appreciate a thank-you note and any suggestions you have. They like to know what interested you most. If the tour guides have been specially helpful, it is genuinely appreciated if you say so.

Because of tight security regulations in some buildings, a few firms have discontinued tours, but there are still many who do give them.

I know more than one woman who got an idea for the kind of training she'd like to take and the kind of job she'd like by going on a tour. Tours help you get the feel of a firm, too. You can tell a good deal by observing closely the people who work for it. If they look grumpy and apathetic, and as if they all wished they were some place else, you can bet this is not a very good place to work. Most firms have a pleasant receptionist out where everyone can see her, but when you get a little farther back behind the scenes sometimes you see a different picture.

You can also get some idea of the climate of a place by the comments employees make about it. Naturally, you won't hear these on a tour, but you will know employees of firms where you think you might like to work. Of course, you must realize that some people are chronic complainers—the kind who demand Utopia by next Friday. So always consider the source of comments and complaints before making a hard judgment.

Chapter 6

What Kinds of Office Jobs Can You Find?

The returning housewife won't find many of the routine office jobs she recalls from the past. The computer has eliminated hundreds of them; but it has also created hundreds of new jobs. The computer doesn't have to intimidate you if you know a little more about it and how it compares to your own thinking processes.

A distinguished mathematician, Louis Robinson, who is the director of standards and systems evaluation in the Systems Development Division of the IBM Corporation, spoke about the past and future applications of computer technology in the business world. He said that no machine yet devised can begin to compare with the most complex computer of them all—the human mind. Computers are composed of up to 100,000 electronic switches, which go either off or on in numerical sequence. There are 13 trillion similar switches in the human mind.

Although the computer as we know it now is little more than twenty years old, it isn't a new machine. In 1833 an Englishman, Charles Babbage, invented what he called "an analytical machine," which was the first automatic digital computer. Associated with Babbage was a mathematical genius, who became the first woman programmer. Daughter of Lord Byron, famed English poet, Lady Lovelace interpreted Babbage's work for the public by describing a form of arithmetic, called *binary,* using only zeros and ones. Today this binary arithmetic is the basic math of computers.

Babbage's machine was never a commercial success, and after

his death no major advances took place in automatic computation until 1937, when Professor Howard Aiken of Harvard University became interested in combining established principles with punch-card concepts. In 1944 an automatic-sequence-controlled calculator named Harvard Mark I was built and formally presented to Harvard. In 1951 the machines became available for commercial application, and now there are said to be more than seventy thousand computers in use in the United States. Although computers are used to some extent in almost all business, industry, and government offices, most are found in six areas: federal government, insurance, banks, aerospace, electrical machinery, and automobiles.

Today over 300,000 persons work as programmers. Many thousands more work as reconcilers, console operators, sorter operators, printer operators, and tape librarians—just to name some of the jobs. Because computers cost millions, they usually run twenty-four hours a day, so shift hours are available.

Programmer jobs are usually considered professional, not clerical, with many firms preferring a college degree. Others require electronic data-processing experience.

For the other electronic data-processing jobs, except possibly that of reconciler, you need electronic data-processing training.

Caution: Check Carefully Before You Enroll in a School

Because the computer has created so many new jobs, electronic data-processing schools have sprung up everywhere. Some are good and some are *worthless.*

Find out whether the school has been accredited by a state regulatory agency and whether it actually has access to computers for students to use (some don't). You cannot learn by mail or without machines to practice on. Ask if the school has placement services and what the experience of recent graduates has been in finding jobs.

Sometimes newspapers run series of articles about the various training schools in the area. These are always helpful to read. Some graduates have been delighted with the training they received.

Others, after spending hundreds of dollars for training, have been sadly disappointed to find that it wasn't adequate to secure programmer jobs, for example.

This is why it is so important to have good advice before you jump into new fields. The divorcee or the widow who is suddenly plunged into the working world especially needs counseling.

High school and other counselors advise their students to see what courses state-supported schools have to offer. Many vocational schools and junior colleges have electronic data-processing courses. To find out what vocational schools there are in your area write to American Vocational Association, 1510 H Street N.W., Washington, D.C., 20005.

Before you enroll in any private business school in your area, whether for data processing, secretarial training, court reporting, or other vocational fields, you can determine the reliability of the school if you check with:

1. The state superintendent of public instruction, whose office has to approve all private schools
2. The Better Business Bureau
3. Major employers in the field that interests you
4. Graduates of the school, for their experience in getting jobs
5. The Veterans Administration (if a veteran)

Further information about careers in electronic data-processing may be obtained from Data Processing Management Association, 505 Busse Highway, Park Ridge, Ill. 60068.

A list of reading materials giving information about computer personnel may be obtained from the Association for Computing Machinery, 1133 Avenue of the Americas, New York, N.Y. 10036.

Other Job Trends

The Occupational Outlook Handbook, published by the Bureau of Labor Statistics, is a helpful guide to show you where job expansion has been the greatest, and where some familiar clerical jobs are decreasing. This book describes:

1. Occupations
2. Nature of the work

3. Places of employment
4. Training and other qualifications needed
5. Outlook for the job
6. Sources of additional information

High school, college, and other counselors use the handbook. Since it is published only about every two years, bear in mind that some salaries quoted are out of date. You will find the book in the reference file of most libraries.

The largest major occupation group of employed women in recent years has been that of clerical workers. Although women's employment in the clerical field has grown continuously, some white-collar jobs are disappearing. Computers are now doing much bookkeeping, payroll, sales, invoicing, and inventory work, especially in the insurance, telephone, department store, and banking industries. As a result there is less demand for such office workers as bookkeepers, payroll clerks, calculating and tabulating machine operators, and file clerks. There are still many openings for key punch operators, but, in offices where they are beginning to install optical scanners, the demand will lessen.

Telephone operators, one very large group of women clerical workers, have been greatly affected by the installation of direct-dialing equipment.

This does not mean that these jobs have all disappeared. You have only to read the want ads to see openings for many of the clerical jobs mentioned above. But it is always a good idea to know which way employment trends are moving.

Facing the Realities of Life

The realities of life include not only getting the right kind of counseling and job training to qualify for current and future job opportunities, but also broadening your job horizons. A growing economy may require several job changes in the course of your working life. You can cope better with changing job demands if you are flexible and willing to train for new jobs.

One big problem with the returning housewife is that she often says, "But I don't want any old routine job. I want an interesting job."

Many of the women who come back to work have not had a wide variety of work experience. Perhaps they got a job rather easily, when they were just out of high school, at a time when office jobs were not as complex as today's. Many often say when you ask what job they held, "Oh, I did a little typing and filing for about a year, and then I got married. My husband didn't want me to work."

You will be competing with women just out of high school and college, women with experience in business courses and with people already on the job, especially for the "interesting jobs."

Without the background and training for any of the new jobs, you will probably have to start with what you know. For many women that means typing. Of the nearly 10 million in clerical jobs, over 3,650,000 million women are working as typists, stenographers, and secretaries. The National Secretaries' Association estimates there are about 1.5 million secretaries in the country, about 2.3 percent of whom are men.

Is Typing a Touchstone or a Trap?

If you are a recent college graduate, you have every right to feel put down if an employer asks, "Can you type?" He wouldn't ask a male graduate the same question. But if you are an older housewife, with rusty skills, and no college training, typing can be a steppingstone. It doesn't have to be a trap unless you let it become one in the future.

The typewriter opened many doors to women about a century ago. Before that they had very little choice of jobs outside the home. The alternative was to slave in a factory for long hours, teach school, or work as a domestic servant. In the United States it wasn't until the Civil War that women were allowed to be nurses.

In the late 1860s Christopher Sholes, Carlos Glidden, and Samuel Soulé of Milwaukee, Wisconsin, helped to develop the first practical typewriter, which was patented in 1869 and, in 1873, the rights to which were sold to E. Remington & Sons. At that time women's work in offices was to fill and haul coal scuttles, sweep floors, and empty spittoons. Men filled all the clerical jobs.

After typewriters appeared in offices, eight brave young women ventured, in 1881, to take a typing class in a New York YWCA.

Employers thundered that the girls would collapse under the strain. Bearded tycoons carried on tirades against "incompetent females with no physical stamina."

But then, as now, fortunately there were some farsighted employers who hired women for what long had been considered "men's jobs." Thus the first white-collar girls appeared in offices heavy with oak furniture and brass cuspidors.

Typing can put you in tune with the modern office, and once there you will find many company-sponsored courses you can take to help your advancement. You will need typing for many of the courses when you write reports, so it is not just for people who want to remain in those jobs, or to become stenographers or secretaries. I agree with a well-known newspaperman who said he thought both boys and girls should learn how to type as soon as they can read and spell.

Later on, I am going to tell you about women who used some of the routine clerical jobs to get back into offices, but who did not let these jobs keep them at the bottom of the ladder. Perhaps there will come a time, as you advance, when it's better not to let on you know how to type. But that time is not when you're trying to get back in after a lapse of twenty years or so.

Typists, stenographers, and secretaries are employed by public and private organizations of every size and type. Public stenographers and some reporting stenographers, such as court reporters, are often self-employed.

Large numbers of stenographers, typists, and secretaries work for government agencies, manufacturing firms, schools and colleges, insurance companies, financial institutions, and hospitals. Many, including technical stenographers and secretaries, are employed in the offices of physicians, attorneys, and other professional people.

To qualify for positions in the federal government and for employment in many private firms, stenographers must be able to take dictation at the rate of at least 80 words a minute and type 40 words a minute or more, with accuracy. Some private firms have lowered the required rate of speed, because of difficulties obtaining more experienced people.

Shorthand reporting requires 200 words a minute or more.

Special Information About Secretaries

The job of secretary varies so much from place to place, and is so often underrated, that one should know more about what it takes to be a really good secretary. Some people refer to anyone who can type and answer the phone competently as a "secretary," a term that is far from accurate in many cases.

To get more information about what is required from a top-notch secretary write to:

National Association of Legal Secretaries, 1312 Fort Worth National Bank Building, Fort Worth, Tex., 76102.

National Secretaries' Association, 1103 Grand Avenue, Suite 410, Kansas City, Mo. 64106.

National Association of Educational Secretaries, 1201 16th Street, N.W., Washington, D.C. 20036.

For information about shorthand reporting as a career write to:

Mr. Robert B. Morse, Executive Secretary, National Shorthand Reporters Association, 25 West Main Street, Madison, Wis. 53703.

Cashiers

Cashiers work for business firms of many types and sizes. More than half are employed in grocery, drug, and other retail stores; large numbers will be found in restaurants, theaters, hotels, and motels. Although most of these establishments and other businesses that employ cashiers are located in cities and in the shopping centers of heavily populated suburban areas, many are also in small towns. Employment in this large occupation is expected to increase very rapidly in the 1970s. Opportunities probably will continue to be best for cashiers having bookkeeping and other special skills, although there will also be broad opportunities for cashiers who wish to work part time.

Cashiering is often sound basic preparation for teller work in financial institutions. More qualifications are required for teller work, but a cashier becomes accustomed to working fast and accurately, both of which are requirements, among others, for the teller job.

Bank Tellers

Some fourteen thousand banks are listed in the United States, and all have teller jobs, even in the smallest towns.

Big banks have schools for tellers with additional training on the job. A bank teller does much more than cash checks and receive deposits. Consequently, after she is trained in the fundamentals, she is given additional courses in sales, so that she will be able to tell customers about other bank services.

An attractive appearance and a good disposition are prime requisites for a teller's job. Maturity can be an asset, too. Since there are numerous part-time teller openings, many women returning to work have, if they have the proper qualifications, found jobs as tellers. And because many banks have branches in the suburbs, these part-time jobs have especially suited women who want to work near home and for less than a full week.

Naturally, when one handles so much money, it is especially important to have good references. Banks check one's credit rating, because if a person cannot handle his own finances, he will hardly be a good prospect for the job!

Because by nature they like to work directly with customers, good tellers indirectly do public relations work for a bank.

Savings and Loan Associations

There are fifty-six hundred savings and loan associations in the United States, both in big cities and in small towns. They, too, have branches in the suburbs with part-time teller jobs, where they often employ housewives. They offer well-designed training programs and good opportunities for advancement.

Office Machine Operators

Office machine operators are employed chiefly in firms handling a large volume of record keeping and other paperwork. Consequently, a great many operators work in the larger cities where such firms are usually located. Approximately one-third of all office machine operators are employed by manufacturing companies. Others work for banks, insurance companies, government agencies, and wholesale and retail firms.

Some office machine operators are employed in "service centers" —agencies that are equipped with various kinds of office machines and contract to handle tasks for other firms without this equipment, such as preparing monthly bills and mailing circulars to lists of prospective customers.

Telephone Operators

There are still many thousands of women employed as telephone operators. Approximately three-fifths work as central operators in telephone companies, and two-fifths as private branch exchange (PBX) operators.

Although **PBX** operators are found in establishments of all kinds, a particularly large number are employed in manufacturing plants, hospitals, schools, and department stores. Jobs for both central office operators and PBX operators tend to be concentrated in heavily populated areas. Nearly one-fifth of the total operators, for example, are employed in the metropolitan areas of New York City, Chicago, and Los Angeles. Practically all the operators are women, although a few men now serve as operators in some sections of the country.

In some small offices the **PBX** job is combined with assignments as receptionist or typist.

The telephone companies not only provide instructions for their own operators, but they will also train **PBX** operators for their customers.

Receptionists

Many women who want to return to work think that if they are not qualified to do anything else they could at least be a receptionist. But being a receptionist is not a simple job, nor is it easy to get a position if you are just returning to work.

It is a very rare office that does not prefer a youngish, attractive girl at the reception desk. In addition to being eye-catching, she must understand the organization thoroughly and know its people. So this is hardly a job for a beginner, young or old, under any circumstances. It is disconcerting to walk into a firm and find that the receptionist cannot answer any of your questions—a situation that is not only poor public relations but has actually lost many a good customer for firms that failed to hire qualified people for this key job.

Minimum Educational Requirements

For all of the foregoing jobs, a high school diploma or its equivalent is usually required. For some, previous experience is necessary, in addition to the required business training.

Many firms will give you tests to see if you have the aptitude for the kinds of office jobs they wish to fill. We'll discuss taking tests in another chapter.

Warning: Be Wary of Work-At-Home Jobs

Year in and year out the Better Business Bureau warns about work-at-home jobs that may lead to bilking. The bureau says that *most* work-at-home jobs are nothing more than a pitch for money. Because so many of these schemes are outright fakes, *always check with the Better Business Bureau before you send any money or get involved!*

Part-Time Temporary Jobs

A good way to see what office jobs are most in demand is to watch the ads of the part-time, temporary-placement service companies. Because there are so many of these companies now, and because the part-time temporary office job has helped many mature women get back into office work, an entire chapter (Chapter 8, pages 81–92) is devoted to this subject.

Chapter 7

Civil Service Jobs
to Consider

Since the government is by far the largest employer in the United States, it may help you to know more about civil service jobs and how to get them.

Let's start with the federal employees. Approximately nine out of ten jobs in the federal government are covered by the Civil Service Act, which the U.S. Civil Service Commission administers.

The act was passed by Congress to ensure that federal employees are hired on the basis of individual merit and fitness. It provides for competitive examinations and the selection of new employees from among those who make the highest scores. The commission, through its network of sixty-five area offices, is responsible for examining and rating applicants and supplying federal departments and agencies with names of persons for the jobs to be filled.

I talked with an area manager of one of the sixty-five Federal Job Information Centers, U.S. Civil Service Commission. He was so interested and enthusiastic having me get information to you that I want to pass on as much I can.

He gave me a booklet, published in February 1971, called "Working for the U.S.A." It has so much good information in it, I urge you to get one from the Federal Job Information Center nearest your home. You will find a list of these centers in the Appendix, page 207.

Did you realize that out of almost 3 million federal employees, only about one-tenth are stationed in Washington, D.C.? If you look in the Yellow Pages under Federal Government, even in a small town you will find names and addresses of many small offices, such as a county office of the Farmer's Home Administration, Department of Agriculture, or an office of the Internal Revenue Service or the Social Security Administration.

California, New York, Pennsylvania, Texas, and Illinois have high concentrations of federal workers. About forty thousand are employed in foreign countries and about twenty thousand in U.S. territories.

Keeping Posted

Your Federal Job Information Center provides information about:
1. All of the current job announcements open in their area and in many other parts of the United States
2. Specific vacancies in shortage categories
3. Opportunities for overseas employment
4. Employment advisory service

These centers are especially equipped to answer all inquiries about federal employment. Since the federal government is the world's largest employer of handicapped people, it has a strong program aimed at their employment. Special provisions are made for the blind and the deaf to take civil service examinations.

Your Post Office Can Help You, Too

To assist the Federal Job Information Center, many post offices also furnish information about current job announcements and give out application forms. If your own post office does not have this information, they should be able to tell you the location of the nearest post office where it may be obtained.

Most states now have a state-wide Wide Area Telephone Service information network, so a person can get federal job information by calling a toll-free number. Just dial 800 555-1212 and ask for the U.S. Civil Service Commission WATS job information number.

Job Announcements

The announcement tells you:

1. What experience or education you must have before your application will be accepted
2. Whether a written test is required
3. Where the jobs are located
4. Rate of pay and salary range on the job
5. Closing date of application

Many offices publish bilingual announcements, if they are in Spanish-speaking areas.

Filing the Application

If you find a job announcement for which you think you qualify, at this time you may have to fill out only a short form, but sooner or later you'll need to fill out a longer form. Be sure to answer every question, because if you do not the area office will have to write to you to get the missing information. This will only delay your application.

The area manager I spoke to pointed out several things you'll be glad to know, among them:

1. You can get credit now for volunteer work you have done under "qualifying experience." You will need a reference from the volunteer agency for which you worked.
2. You can get extra points on your test score if you are a veteran, widow or widower of a veteran, or wife of a disabled veteran. You will need to have proof of these circumstances.

For further information about veteran preference ask your Federal Job Center for Pamphlet BRE-48, *Opportunities in the Federal Service for Veterans.*

After you file your application you may need to take a written test; you will receive a notice through the mail telling you where and when to report for the test.

All Federal Job Information Centers have examining points throughout the state, so that everyone will easily be able to get to a nearby point.

How You Can Help Yourself Prepare for the Test

When you are applying for a civil service job, it is well to bear in mind that civil service is based on the merit system. Since persons already on the staff will probably be promoted to higher ranking jobs, you will usually have to compete for those open at a lower level.

Because there are usually many clerical openings, I am including, in the Appendix, p. 219, a sample of the test given typists and stenographers. It will help you a great deal to practice with this test, because it is similar to tests given in private firms.

The area manager cautioned against schools that promise or imply that they can get you a civil service job, since *no one* can guarantee to do that for you. But he did recommend books published by several firms that do help people pass civil service tests. Usually priced under $5.00, they are available in most libraries at the readers' service desk, where all the civil service books are filed in one place. If they are not available there ask the librarian to get the books for you on the interlibrary loan system. These books will not only help prepare you for civil service tests, but also for jobs in private firms.

In addition to job announcements, samples of civil service applications, tests, and detailed descriptions of jobs are included. The books also give good information about study techniques, which you can apply to any course you may be taking.

The area manager suggested you give yourself plenty of time to get to the examining point, so that you won't arrive all breathless and flustered. If need be, time yourself beforehand if you're not sure how long it will take you to get there. If you are late, you will not be admitted to the examination.

He thought you might be interested to know that the range of jobs in the federal government covers almost every kind of job found in private industry. The libraries which are federal depositories are required to keep all the current government publications on file. A small library would not have room for all of them, but many libraries have the *United States Government Organization Manual*. In its over eight hundred pages, you can learn a great deal about all segments of the government.

After You Have Taken the Tests

You will be notified whether you qualified in the examination by the area office that announced it. You should look on the back of your rating notice to see how long your eligibility extends, which will be from three months to one year. When it expires, you may write to your area office to be reinstated.

If you are found to be one of the top three best qualified for the job, your name will be referred to an agency for possible employment and you'll be contacted to see if you are available and may be called in for an interview. From these interviews, the agency will select the person who seems best suited for the job.

If there is a federal institution in your city such as a hospital, laboratory, and so on, usually after you have obtained civil service eligibility, you may also apply there directly, since most have their own personnel departments.

Other Civil Service Jobs

If you are interested in state, county, or city civil service jobs, the state employment service will give you the needed information about openings. Job announcements may be posted in the post office and in many libraries. Sometimes these job announcements for typing and stenography will tell you whether the test will be given on a manual or electric typewriter, so you can prepare properly.

These job announcements are interesting to study because they will give you up-to-date information about job descriptions, salary ranges, and qualifications. A study of the announcements may suggest to you something you never thought of doing, but for which you may be qualified.

Outlook for Civil Service Jobs

The Occupational Outlook Handbook, 1970–1971 edition, says:

Government employment has grown faster than any other industry division, and has more than doubled from 5.5 million to 11.8 million between 1947 and 1968.

Growth has been mostly at the State and local levels. . . . Government will continue to be a major source of new jobs through the 1970's. Most of the growth will continue to be in the State and local governments.

Some libraries have the quarterly magazine called the *Civil Service Journal,* published by the Civil Service Commission. In it you will find interesting articles and up-to-date information about the civil service.

A job hunt may be discouraging at times, but it does start a person thinking about ways to get out of a rut. Reading is one of the best ways to help yourself.

Chapter 8

"Temporary" May Be Your Best Answer

"I went back to work at sixty-five, after just one month of retirement, because I was bored to death."

But who will hire a woman sixty-five years old, you may wonder.

If you have a readily marketable office skill, no matter what your age, consider the temporary placement office services.

What Is Temporary Help Service?

The temporary help contractor is not an employment agency. Temporary workers are on the payroll of the temporary service firm for whom they work. There is no fee to pay. Temporaries are paid the prevailing rate within the community where the temporary assignment is done. You are paid directly by your temporary help service employer.

The client is billed a service charge, which covers the direct costs for the hours you work plus indirect costs for which the temporary help service is responsible, including social security, workmen's compensation, bonding, and payroll taxes.

Temporary help services started shortly after World War II, when several firms offered help to corporations who wanted to lease personnel rather than put extra temporary help on their own payroll.

In the past twenty-five years, the business has had a phenomenal growth. The number of firms in the industry has grown from a few to hundreds, many with nationwide offices as well as offices outside the United States.

Who Works for Temporary Help Service Offices?

Although an increasing number of men are employed for jobs in industry by these firms, estimates say 75 percent of their employees are women, many of whom fall into the following categories:

Housewives

Temporary help services can be the answer to many problems posed by the demands of home and children and the desire to work. Let some of the housewives speak for themselves:

"I can work thirty hours a week, and no one gets annoyed at me if I take the summer off when the children are out of school."

"I can choose the days I want to work. Mother will baby-sit, but doesn't want to do it more than two days a week."

"I can choose jobs near my home."

"My husband doesn't mind if I work, but since his job involves a good deal of traveling, he doesn't want me to be tied down all the time. He likes to have me go with him sometimes, without much advance notice."

"My husband is transferred often, so I can't take a permanent job right now. The temporary help service I work for has offices in many cities. When we move to a new city, I can work for the office there."

Job transfers are frequent for men between the ages of twenty-five and thirty-eight. Among the transferred workers, the frequency of the shift comes every two and a half years now, compared with every five years a decade ago. Among those transferred are not predominantly highly paid executives but are in those salary brackets where the wife is likely to go to work.

"My husband is laid off from work sometimes. When that happens, I go to work to help out."

"I used to be a secretary, and I really don't need the income, but I want to keep up my skills so if the occasion arises I'll be ready to take a full-time job. Working a few days a week suits me very well."

"When I decided to go back to work, I didn't really know exactly what I wanted to do, or what kind of office I wanted to work in. Working for a temporary help service has given me a fine variety of experience and has helped me decide where I want to work full time eventually."

"I want to get a degree, but there isn't enough money for the children's tuition and mine, too. I work a few days to help pay my tuition while I take courses. Eventually I'll be prepared for a higher-paying job."

"I was tired of volunteer work, but I don't want a full-time, year-round job. I just like to get out where the action is and have something new to talk about."

"We want to take a really interesting vacation this year. I work temporarily to help pay for it."

"We have such high medical bills, I must work to help out, but I can't be away from home too much."

"I like working for a temporary help service, because I don't need a big wardrobe. Since I work in many different offices, no one knows I'm wearing the same clothes over and over."

Students and Teachers

Students over eighteen and teachers sometimes work for temporary help services during vacations. Some students who are just out of school prefer to sample a number of jobs before deciding on a career.

Full-Time Workers Between Jobs

Some full-time workers between jobs want to explore new fields and earn money while looking for permanent work.

For example, let's say you have just moved from New York City to Chicago. You've never been in the Middle West. You know nothing about the city or the job opportunities. There may not be anything open at your level, so rather than take a lesser job, you may find it expedient to work for a temporary help service while you become acquainted with the city.

There are some young, unattached women who work for temporary help offices because they like to travel and don't want to stay in any city too long a time.

Retired Persons

Inflation takes such a huge bite out of fixed incomes, you may want to supplement your pension and social security.

Many persons dream of the time when they will have "nothing to do," but one has only to look at many retired persons, whether they have retired from a job in business, or whether they are housewives who have completed rearing children to adulthood, to realize how bored many are when they really have "nothing to do."

Age is not a barrier in working for a temporary help service. Indeed, one such firm specializes in hiring mature workers, both men and women. It has offices principally in the East, on the West Coast, and one in Chicago, Illinois.

The manager of one office said, "We try to place everyone we consider qualified. What we look for are women who are reliable, stable, experienced, and, most important, with high-level skills. This does not mean that every older woman automatically qualifies, nor that every younger woman does not. What it does mean is we interview everyone and hire a few, regardless of age, and we hire qualified persons."

Since many applicants may have been out of work for some time and may be jittery about returning, a number of the interviewers are retirees themselves. Many were either teachers or personnel workers.

Many of the other temporary help services hire older women, too. I recall one retired woman, well into her sixties, who was invaluable at tax time because of her past experience. Not only could she do twice as much work as many eighteen-year-olds, but it was always accurate.

A New York manager remarked after an unusually bad blizzard there, "When we have a storm like this, our *older* temporary workers *always* come to work. It's the young ones who use the weather as an excuse to stay home."

Being set in one's ways is supposed to be characteristic of old age, but chronological age is not the key to this trait. Some eighteen-year-old workers become terribly upset if they cannot have lunch and coffee breaks at *exactly* the same time as their girl friends. This type of girl often lacks flexibility. She wants to sit at exactly the same desk, at exactly the same hours every day.

A high degree of flexibility is important for temporary help, who must go from job to job on short notice. Temporary help service offices will tell you that a good many older workers have this valuable trait. Popping in and out of jobs, too, calls for more than average ability. One manager said, "One of my best stenographers is sixty-eight years old. She doesn't mind at all driving her own car to many different assignments. She seems to thrive on the change of pace."

What to Expect When You Register at a Temporary Help Service

To find such services look in your classified directories under "Temporary Help Contractors or Employment Contractors—Temporary Help."

In big cities such as New York as many as eight to fifteen pages will be required to list the temporary help services. Some are local only, but many are nationwide, a factor which can be valuable if you will be moving to another city. Even in fairly small towns you'll find temporary help services.

It's a good idea to study the ads in the Yellow Pages, because these firms are not all alike; some, not many, are also employment agencies.

After you register—and, remember, there is no fee for registering—you'll be interviewed, tested, and classified according to skills, experience, working days, and location preferred. Be sure to tell the interviewer if you can write and speak more than one language.

One of my favorite temporary help service managers said, "We never scare the housewives by saying we're going to give them some tests. We just tell them we'd like a sample of their work."

Many persons freeze the moment you mention the word "tests," so I've always liked that "work sampling" approach.

In many of the firms such a test would include a quiz for accuracy—matching names and numbers, for example. Shorthand, typing, dictating machine, adding machine, and spelling tests are some of the most frequently given, depending, of course, on the type of position you are seeking.

What Jobs Are Most in Demand?

Typists usually head the list, followed by:
> Stenographers
> Dictation machine operators
> Key punch operators
> General office workers
> File clerks

Other jobs include:
> Telephone solicitation (a good telephone voice is a great asset in many office jobs)
> Stuffing envelopes
> Doing copy work
> Serving as a messenger
> Operating a switchboard
> Demonstrating products or services
> Making market surveys

Naturally there are other job classifications, such as teachers to work on research projects, but the ones mentioned above are the most usual in calls for temporary office help. And remember that small offices are most likely to use a combination of skills on job orders.

As more people learn data processing, some firms furnish temporary office help for those jobs, too.

What If Your Skills Are Out of Date?

If you are accurate on details, you could start in a file job. In the meantime, if you once had typing and had used other office machines, some of the temporary help services will offer you a chance to use an electric typewriter and teach you how to use other office machines. Others let you practice on the office machines they have available without charge.

Some have a training director, excellent training manuals, and an employees' newsletter to help you.

Since the temporary help services are not all alike in size or operation, be sure to find out about opportunities to bring your skills up to date.

What About Salaries?

Just as in full-time jobs with one employer, rates of pay will vary with your skills and years of experience. The rate increases in proportion to job skills. You may start out with the simplest kind of job, but, as your rusty talents improve, your pay rate will go up. A woman who has several skills is fortunate, since often the rate is based on the number of assignments she can fill and the hours of work she accumulates.

Some of the temporary help firms send rating cards to the clients they serve. All check by phone to see if the woman's job performance is satisfactory. A rate may be increased because of good on-the-job performance rating.

When quoting salaries today, most firms will tell you what the pay range is and how often they make salary reviews.

If you are hired, you won't need to visit the office every time you get an assignment. Your representative (and be sure to get her name) will telephone you about available jobs in the location you select and for the days you want to work. Of course, if you are willing to work in more than one location, like the sixty-eight-year-old stenographer I described, you will probably get more assignments.

If you practice your office skills at home, be sure to tell your temporary service employer you feel you are ready for more varied assignments. Then you can go back to the firm's office to take more tests. If your skills prove to be sharper, you can expect better assignments and a higher rate of pay.

Before you are sent on an assignment, the service will brief you about the things you will need to know, such as keeping records of your time, when to send in your time reports, when you get paid, required tax deductions, and work policies at a client's office. All firms stress how vitally important it is to be sure all your work is kept *confidential!* You must not discuss what you have typed in Client A's office when you go to Client B's office. Your representative will also explain the procedure for reporting illness, injury, emergency, or any unusual event that occurs on a work assignment. Always call the temporary help service about these matters, not the client.

Keep in mind that many assignments are for emergency help. I had the experience of asking for a typist to fill an urgent and immediate need, only to have her not show up. She called me much later to say, "I'm snowed in." If you're delayed or incapacitated unexpectedly don't call the client. Call the temporary help service at once so the manager can hop right to it to find someone else. Otherwise, the annoyed client is likely to use another temporary help service the next time there is a rush call for help.

When a client calls in an order for, let's say, a typist, your representative will find out if the work is to be done on an electric or manual typewriter, whether it is light typing or in volume, what the hours are, how long the assignment will last, the person to report to, the exact address of the firm, and as much about the job as possible. Don't trust your memory. Write down all of these facts. Since many firms have branch offices, be sure you report to the right one.

Your temporary help service will give you an introductory card to hand to the person you report to.

Why Do Employers Use Temporary Help Services?

1. For emergencies. When extra work arises unexpectedly, it takes time and money to find an experienced worker, and requires all the red tape of putting her on the payroll. When an organization needs someone for just a few days, or even a few weeks, it is often easier and less expensive to let a temporary help service handle the red tape.

For a rush job, studies have shown that temporary employees often work more efficiently and productively than permanent employees. The temporary worker is not apt to be distracted by in-company cliques, and thus does not feel motivated to spend time on the job getting the latest office scuttlebutt.

2. For covering shortness of help. During vacation periods, or when several people are unexpectedly ill at the same time, organizations need help. The same situation might be true during a time when the labor market in general is tight, or when there is a shortage of people with certain skills and experience. It is then better in many cases to turn to temporary services rather than try to make do with people not fully qualified.

3. For recurring seasonal peak-load jobs.

4. For special projects, such as market surveys, sales campaigns, direct mail programs, staffing booths at conventions, or demonstrating products in stores.

It is said the temporary help services now provide skills in more than 125 job classifications. (This includes men, of course.) But most requests are for white-collar temporary employees.

Advantages and Benefits of Temporary Employment

1. Flexibility of hours and location of work.

2. Some of the firms now offer the temporary worker paid vacations.

3. Some offer a bonus to people on their active list if they can bring in a new, qualified worker who is hired and works at least three hundred hours for the service.

4. No age barrier. This is an important advantage, since more than 600,000 women over sixty-five are in the labor force. Many of them can tell you they are delighted to know that there are places where age will not bar them if they are otherwise qualified for the jobs.

5. The opportunity of working on different kinds of jobs.

What To Observe About Offices
When You Are on Assignment

When you go on a new job, especially to meet an emergency, you can expect things to be a little hectic. Still, you can tell a good deal about an office by the way the supervisors treat the temporary help—or any employee, for that matter.

Some offices really do not get their full value from temporary help because they fail to observe a few simple rules:

1. The manager must inform the regular staff that a temporary worker will be there for a few days, or whatever the time is. Otherwise, some permanent employees may make the temporary feel like an intruder competing for their jobs.

2. Facilities must be made ready. Temporary help services try to find employees who can settle right down and pitch in. Thus, it is aggravating for a temporary to arrive on a job only to find that the firm has not carefully preplanned for her arrival and has failed to have equipment ready. Time and money are wasted if someone has to rush around to locate a typewriter, paper, carbon, eraser, or other materials.

3. The nature of the work must be adequately described. You can do a far better job if the supervisor explains what is needed, even if you are only stuffing envelopes or typing names on cards. Work is more meaningful when you know *why* you're doing something and *why* the deadline is so important.

Some managers can make the most routine job sound like an important part of the day's function, while others, unhappily, make a person feel little better than an office machine.

One woman told me, "I knew my temporary job was not world-shaking, but it's nice to be treated like a human being. I really felt good when the supervisor said, 'We're so glad you came to help us out.' "

4. A "buddy" should be assigned to make you feel comfortable. After you meet the supervisor, it helps to be assigned to someone to introduce you to fellow workers, show you where to keep your coat and where the rest room is, and tell you what time your lunch hour will be (thirty minutes is the usual time allotted for temporary workers). Many firms also give you coffee breaks at the same time as the regular staff. The thoughtful firms will have someone go with you for lunch and coffee breaks on your first day and will also remember that temporary workers like to be called by name. Also, write down the names of the persons you'll need to ask for further

information and to check your work periodically to be sure you have understood all aspects of it.

5. A capable manager will have given your temporary help service a good job description of the work you are to do. But sometimes you'll find a manager who has asked for a top-notch stenographer when all he needs is someone to type names on file cards, do some copy work, and maybe write two letters in four days! This will cost the client money, since experienced stenographers get much higher rates than routine typists. This kind of goof can make you wonder whether the manager really does know what the jobs in his office involve! A good manager never throws money away needlessly because of failure to keep adequate job descriptions in the office.

Disadvantages of Working for a Temporary Help Service

1. There are seldom fringe benefits such as one usually finds in most regular full-time jobs: life and health insurance, paid vacations, pension, sick leave, and the like.

2. There is less opportunity for advancement.

3. Some temporaries eventually find that they tire of going different places and prefer settling in a permanent part-time or full-time job. There are year-round part-time jobs in some firms today, but some temporary help services find little call for people who can work only part of the day. Since this is not true of all temporary help services, it is well to inquire.

4. You can seldom practice on the job in the office you're sent to. When a client needs temporary help, he expects someone who is fully trained. If you can't do the work, he has every right to call the temporary service to substitute someone else right away. However, clients are expected to pay a temporary worker for at least four hours if she reports for work—even if the client later finds she does not fill the bill. In this case, the client does not have to *keep* you there four hours, but you'll be paid for four hours, even if you stay only one hour.

In spite of the few disadvantages, the temporary help service has reintroduced thousands of housewives to the business world. Many clients use favorite temporary help services because their employees consistently do outstanding work. Often clients will ask for the same woman upon every occasion when they need someone with her qualifications. I recall one woman who knew so many different jobs in one department that every time a special project came up or disaster struck in an emergency, the manager would phone to say, "Please call XYZ Temporary Help Service and say we need Mrs. G. as soon as possible."

When a temporary help service hires you, the firm must protect itself from having clients try to hire you full time. So it usually requires anywhere from sixty to ninety days' notice before you can leave to go to work for a client who wants to put you on his permanent payroll. Some require the client to pay a fee if he wants to hire you.

These firms have filled a real purpose for thousands of clients, often tiding them over some very rough spots when there was a need to meet special projects, critical staff shortages, seasonal work, and emergency jobs.

I think many of you may find the temporary help service an answer to your first steps back to the business world. These services usually seem to have a special understanding of the housewife who wants to go back to work.

Chapter 9

The Interview—How to Come Out Ahead

The day has arrived—you have an appointment for an interview. If you are nervous, you have lots of company.

Because so many women coming back to work were married in their teens, they may never have applied for a job since the first one they held just after high school graduation. Or, as some widows and divorcees have told me, "I got married when I was eighteen and never worked outside the home. This is the first time I've *ever* applied for a job." No wonder some women feel as though they are entering a torture chamber when they go for their first interview. Yet it does not have to be an ordeal at all.

Some Facts That May Help You

1. Go back to Chapter 3 and review the advance preparation mentioned because this will truly build your confidence. Before you go into the interview, simply list a few main reasons why you feel you are qualified for the job. Then keep these thoughts uppermost in your mind. Remember, the employer is not a mind reader. Moreover, he wants you to stress the qualifications you bring to the job, such as:

      Skills—both natural and acquired

      Personality and appearance

      Educational background

      Work record and habits

      Character and attitudes

How do these match the job requirements? The interviewer tries to see the applicant not only as she is now, but how she will be on the job. Sometimes it helps to say to yourself, "Would I hire myself under these circumstances?" "What would I like to know about me as an applicant?" Think about how you relate to the prospective job. Bolster your confidence by focusing on your qualifications rather than on weaknesses or mistakes you might make.

2. Be on time for the interview. When you are used to working at your own pace at home, it isn't always easy to become time conscious. Since the business world moves by the clock, you may need to make adjustments.

3. Avoid making more than two applications in one day—and not too close together. You never know how long the interview and testing will take. Also, you may be asked to see a department head, as well as the personnel interviewer. If you are answering an ad, there may be many other applicants there, and you will have to wait your turn.

It is only fair to tell you, though, that some interviews do not last very long. Many offices have a fact-screening interview. If for example, the job hours call for 8:30 A.M. to 5:00 P.M., and you say, "I can only work from 9:00 A.M. to 4:00 P.M." that may end the interview. Or if you say, "I can't start until after my husband's vacation," that could also be the end of the interview, since most firms want to hire someone as soon as possible.

4. Avoid sandwiching interviews between shopping trips. Bundles are a nuisance. You can't expect the receptionist to keep an eye on them for you, nor will you want to go to the interviewer's office all loaded down with excess baggage.

5. Do a little advance research. The employer is going to try to find out if you are a suitable applicant for his opening. Likewise, you should do some information gathering about the employer. If you know people who worked there, get clues from them. Bear in mind, though, that not everyone has the same opinion about a firm.

There are a number of publications, which can be located in any good-sized college or public library, that can help you learn something about larger firms. Ask the librarian at the reader's service desk to help you find this information. Also, some personnel departments leave annual reports or company publications on the reception room table. Take a look at these while you wait.

Persons and agencies who have given you job leads can also tell you facts about the firm. Whatever you do, don't go in "cold," not knowing a thing about your prospective employer. You don't want to work for someone you don't know anything about, do you?

6. Avoid negatives. If you answer an ad, don't call up and say, "I haven't worked for fifteen years. Do you think I could fill the job you have advertised?" You may think this never happens, but it does. Always go in person to apply for the job—and be enthusiastic. The interview is your chance to *show* that you're the person for the job.

7. If you cannot keep an appointment, have the courtesy to cancel it. If someone has given you an introduction for an interview, don't cancel unless something catastrophic has happened. It is embarrassing for the person recommending someone for a job when the applicant is a "no show."

Some women cancel out because they get nervous. One woman who was tempted to do this said, "Well, I had to make up my mind whether I wanted to act like a grown-up woman or a pampered little girl. So I went for the interview."

8. Go alone to the interview. The employer is interested in you, not in what your friends or relatives have to say about you. Although some women, to bolster their courage, go in pairs, this is never a good idea. You will only be embarrassed if one of you is hired and the other isn't.

Never take small children with you. They will be restless, want to find out how a typewriter works, romp around, and ultimately insist that they either "want to go to the bathroom, Mama" or "want to go home." The presence of small children makes the employer wonder how you could possibly work if you can't find someone to stay with them just during the brief time it takes to look for a job.

Things to Bring with You

1. A pen. Personnel offices furnish pens, but sometimes they are scratchy or go dry at the wrong moments. Also, you would surely prefer to use your own.

2. Your social security card. If you do not have one, apply for one at the local district office of the Social Security Administration before you go on a job interview.

3. Glasses, if needed.

4. A hearing aid, if you wear one.

5. Your résumé, preferably several copies.

6. Discharge papers, if you have been in the armed services.

7. A notebook, since you may be asked to jot down information. Make notes right after your interview, especially if you have more than one interview that day. Since it is easy to forget who offered what about salary, benefits, hours of work, and so on, you'll want to have this specific information when you get home to decide on a choice, if you have one.

8. Reference letters? Bring them if you like, although most employers want to make their own reference checks.

9. Card or letter of introduction. If a friend or business acquaintance has arranged the interview, be sure to bring the written introduction the person has given you. If such a person has phoned to introduce you and you don't have a card, remind the receptionist of this when you stop at the application desk.

Always be polite to the receptionist or secretary in the outer office, no matter whom you know in the company. It never pays to be snooty or to underrate the opinion of a receptionist or secretary, who may say when bringing your application to the personnel director, "This one is a real creep."

Filling Out the Application Blank

Some people do not have kindly thoughts about application blanks.

One applicant said, "My mind goes blank when I see one." Another said, "I wish someone would give a class on filling out forms. I never know what to do with all those questions." Still another took a really belligerent attitude. "I *refuse* to fill them out."

This is hardly a reasonable attitude to take. If there are twenty-five people waiting to be interviewed, why should one be an exception? The employer *has* to have specific information to determine an applicant's qualifications, and the face-to-face interview, as a rule, should not be spent getting routine information that can easily be presented on an application blank.

In any case, practices vary in different companies. Many give you just a short form to fill out for the screening interview.

Suggestions to Help You Fill Out Applications

1. Don't start filling spaces until you have read over the whole application.

2. Before you begin writing, look for the blanks that might be crowded if you have to provide a long answer. If you have a large handwriting, practice writing your answers in a smaller hand on your note pad. It *is* important to have the application form look neat and legible.

3. Be accurate about dates.
    a. Date you fill out the application. Many firms keep their applications for as long as a year but seldom longer.
    b. Dates of service with former employers. You will surely have that written down in advance on your résumé, along with addresses, names of references, and telephone numbers.
    c. Date of birth. This entry makes most women cringe. You cannot hedge about your age to an employer or the Social Security Administration.

This is a bit of a digression, but after you are on a payroll forget the subject of your age. It doesn't pay to go around "talking old." And the personnel department is *never* supposed to reveal age or any other personal information to outsiders.

4. Be careful about spelling. I recall with horror the woman who wrote under Position Desired the following: "Exuative secertery." And then there was the case of a woman who had worked ten years for a well-known firm but spelled the firm's name wrong in every reference to it.

5. When listing former jobs, as on your résumé, always put *the most recent one* at the *top* of the list. Women ask, "What if you haven't worked for twenty years?" Put it down anyway. You

can still help yourself by the way you answer this query. If you started as a file clerk and ended your service as a secretary or supervisor, for example, this shows you have potential for advancement. An application form is no place to be modest, so be sure to *list anything that shows progress.*

If you have had a volunteer job, list that, and if you started as a regular and wound up as a director of volunteers, say so.

If you worked for a temporary help service and were asked frequently to work at the same firm, include that information.

6. "Reasons for leaving former jobs" is a category usually requested on application blanks. Think carefully about your replies. If you answer "Didn't like the work" after several former jobs, this may sound as though you don't like work—period! It never pays to knock a former employer.

If asked whether you've ever been fired and your answer is "Yes," you may wish to explain this in the interview rather than try to write an explanation.

Some firms will ask whether you've ever been arrested. If you have been, you may wish to explain this, too, rather than write the answer.

7. What should you write about salary? You might well remark, "When they ask what salary I received twenty years ago, it looks like peanuts today." But interviewers realize full well that inflation makes it impossible to compare today's salaries with those of the past. If there are questions where you feel that the answer is meaningless, don't leave the space blank, but enter a dash or question mark. You can explain this in the interview.

Since application forms request that you state the job you're seeking and the salary desired, your previous study of salary ranges in the community will pay off. If you prefer to skip the salary question until you have the interview, you can write "open" in the salary blank.

8. Be *sure* to list recent brushup courses you have taken. I cannot emphasize too often how important they are, and how much they do to offset other questions you may dread answering. If you have had a recent course in data processing, for example, you will undoubtedly know *more* about the subject than many women who are working at the firm. People in steady jobs often get in ruts and

put off preparing for the future by learning new skills. (Then they complain when knowledgeable outsiders are hired to fill some of the jobs.)

The Interview

When the receptionist or secretary takes you to meet the interviewer, she should introduce you. Let's hope she doesn't mumble names. If she does, look for the interviewer's name on the door or on a desk name plate. The receptionist will have given your application to the interviewer in advance, although, if it's a small office, maybe you'll just hand it to the interviewer yourself. State your name confidently as you introduce yourself.

A cheerful smile helps to radiate confidence, and it is surely a cheering sight to an interviewer, who may be frazzled after having interviewed a long line of applicants.

No reputable employer would hire a person just on a first impression, but first impressions do tell a good deal about a person.

I've interviewed thousands of persons, and like many personnel colleagues, have found there is nothing more discouraging than to have an applicant slouch in, plop down in a chair with the attitude, "Well, here I am. What can you do for me?" To make it worse, some of these people dump shopping parcels and purses on the interviewer's desk.

Equally unwelcome is the widow who comes in sobbing mournfully, "I don't know what I can do, but I hope you can suggest something! I'll do anything if you'll just give me a chance."

No employer has a job listing for "just anything." It would be helpful to you to know what is going through an interviewer's mind during an interview.

There Is a Specific Job to Fill

Whether the office is large or small, the manager is probably pleading, *"When* are you going to fill this job? You know we don't have all month to train someone for it."

In the larger firms the personnel department receives a requisition which may look like this:

Date Filed _____   REQUISITION FOR PERSONNEL   Date Filled _____

IMPORTANT: Before submitting this requisition, investigate to see if the job can be eliminated or the work
assigned to others to eliminate the need for replacing personnel or adding to your staff.

1. PLEASE PROVIDE: □ PART TIME   □ FULL TIME

BY: _____   HOURS TO BE WORKED: _____
    (Month)   (Day)   (Year)

2. FOR POSITION OF: _____ Job Title _____
   (If this is an entirely new job, so indicate and a job description will be written.)

   □ NEW JOB   □ EXISTING JOB   If Existing Job, indicate:

   _____ Class Number
   _____ Job Description Number

   Special Skills, Abilities or Other Requirements: _____
   _____
   _____
   _____

3. REASON FOR REQUEST

   a. Temporary, for about _____ months.
   b. Addition to staff.
   c. Replacement for _____
      who has been □ terminated □ transferred.
      If transferred, to what description number _____

   Requested For: _____
                  (Responsibility Area)

   Requested By: _____
                 (Responsibility Area Mgr.)

   Approved By: _____
                (Div. Head)

Not all job interview procedures are alike, by any means. In a small office you may be interviewed by the owner or manager, or maybe have a preliminary talk with the manager's secretary. In larger offices, you will go to a personnel department where you may have a screening interview before you reach the person whose job it is to put applicants on the payroll.

Not all interviewers are alike either, but basically there are three parts to every interview:

Establishing Rapport with the Applicant

All firms would like to be known as "a good place to work." Yet it is surprising to find how many companies invest substantially in advertising, then throw goodwill away in the personnel department. Employers aware of good public relations are not going to slam the door in your face, since every job applicant who enters their door may at least be a potential customer for goods or services. The treatment of job applicants can build up or tear down a firm's reputation in the community.

A few interviewers plunge right into an interview with questions such as "What can I do for you?" or "Why do you want to work for us?" or "Tell me about yourself." It is not easy to answer questions like this on a moment's notice. Although some interviewers say they do this to watch the applicant's reactions, most personnel authorities feel that it is more productive to put an applicant at ease.

Personally, I have always felt that the applicant has enough to feel nervous about, and should not be pounced on in this manner. Obviously, it is impossible to hire everyone who applies for jobs. But as one well-known personnel director said, "If the applicant can't walk away feeling good about herself—whether she's right for the job or not—you've failed as an interviewer."

Giving Information to the Applicant

A good interviewer will always try to make you feel comfortable during the first few moments of the interview. Often an applicant has had to wait her turn for an interview. More than likely, during this time she will have gone over in her mind what she's going to say and what the interviewer will be like, or asked herself why she ever applied in the first place. By the time she is ushered into the interviewer's office, her head will be buzzing. If the interviewer does not take a few minutes to help her relax, the applicant won't absorb much of what the interviewer is trying to tell her.

None of us is as skilled about *listening* as we should be, at best, so right here is a good place to say something about this.

Hundreds of books have been published about speaking—few about listening. Dr. Ralph G. Nichols, at the University of Minnesota, made exhaustive studies on listening. Some of his work has been reprinted in a booklet called "Listening Is a Ten Part Skill".*

Says Dr. Nichols:

Most of us spend a good share of our lives listening. Success or failure throughout life is often dependent on how well or how poorly we listen. Almost any job involves a certain amount of listening— listening to instructions for doing it, if nothing else.

Tests of listening comprehension show that without training, the average person listens at about 25 per cent efficiency. This low rating becomes even more deplorable as evidence accumulates that it can be very much raised through training. . . . Work at listening.

One of the most striking characteristics of poor listeners is their disinclination to spend any energy in a listening situation. . . . Listening is hard work. It is characterized by faster heart action, quicker circulation of the blood, a small rise in bodily temperature. The overrelaxed listener is merely appearing to tune in. . . .

For selfish reasons alone one of the best investments we can make is to give each speaker our conscious attention. We ought to establish eye contact and maintain it; to indicate by posture and facial expression that the occasion and the speaker's efforts are a matter of real concern. . . .

Inexperience is not easily or quickly overcome. However, knowledge of our own weakness may lead us to repair it. We need *never become too old to meet new challenges.*

I have heard Dr. Nichols speak and I've taken one of his courses in listening. I commend his book to you, because listening is such an important part of getting a job and holding it. And how about

* Enterprise Publications, 20 North Wacker Drive, Chicago, Ill. 60606; 35¢.

our own families? How often have we heard one of them say, "You're not listening to me."

Among the elements that should be discussed when you're being considered for a job are:

1. Job title and department it is in
2. Purpose of the job
3. Hours to be worked
4. Equipment to be used
5. Responsibilities for handling money, valuables, or confidential data
6. Advancement and promotion policies
7. Type of contact with others
8. General duties
9. Size of department
10. Nature of supervision
11. Benefits
12. Training provided on the job
13. Special tests required
14. Union membership availability
15. Salary range, both at start and later

Some interviewers talk too much, overlooking the fact that it is as important for them to listen as it is for you. Many oversell the job, even knowing that it is better if the applicant realizes not only the advantages but also some of the disadvantages.

Some interviewers hardly talk at all—and they are the hardest to cope with.

Getting Information from the Applicant

A. Whatever you do, *never* apologize for your age, sex, or race. You would be surprised to know how many women start out feebly by saying, "I suppose you think I'm too old for this job."

B. Human dignity is very important. Never demean yourself by pleading for the job. This will turn an interviewer off—fast! Leave family troubles at home. A sob story will kill your chances for the job.

C. Although good interviewers make allowances for nervousness, try to control disconcerting actions like twisting a handkerchief, jiggling your necklace or turning your charm bracelet. When an applicant scarcely says a word but "Yes" or "No," the clam approach makes rough going for the interviewer, who then has to pry out every word of information.

D. Remember again those points you were going to stress about your qualifications for the job. Concentrate on them, and speak out!

E. The interviewer may ask, "What do you want to be doing five years from now?" because employers are interested in your long-term motivation for working. Sometimes they ask, too, what you liked best or what you liked least about your former jobs. Answer such questions directly, but don't go into an endless monologue. And remember an old army rule: "Don't volunteer information you've not been asked for—unless you like trouble."

F. If you have young children, be sure you have planned well in advance how they will be cared for while you are at work. Employers are concerned about this, and want to avoid opening themselves up to disruptive situations.

G. It is always a real joy to interview an enthusiastic person. Henry Thoreau said, "None is so old as the person who has outlived enthusiasm." Enthusiasm is a positive trait that you can cultivate easily.

H. Many women ask, "What will I say when the interviewer asks how much salary I want?" The interviewer knows what job classifications are to be filled and just what the salary ranges are. Where you may fit into that range depends on your qualifications. Salary is often uppermost in the applicant's mind. In fact, many wish that the interviewer would start right out and say, "This job pays this much."

In the long run, though, it is better for you not to have salary discussed first thing. Employers want to know more about you before discussing figures. They can indicate the salary range, but it is hardly fair to either party to take one look at an application, have a short interview, and settle on an exact salary without references from former employers, testing of skills, and taking other steps to determine abilities.

Unhappily, there are still too many businessmen who counter

an applicant's disappointment over the offered amount with, "This is a pretty good salary for a woman."

They forget that millions of women work to support families, aged parents, invalid husbands, and that for many reasons money is just as important to women as it is to men. This is one of the myths that dies hard, but let us hope it can be laid to rest soon, along with many other fables about working women.

There are several replies you can make to the salary question, such as: "What do you *usually* pay for this job?" or "What does this job usually pay to someone with *my qualifications?*" or "It's not just a question of what I want. What do you think I'd be *worth* to your firm?"

Best of all, if you've done your homework on salary ranges for similar jobs in the community by studying want ads, learning from the state employment service, querying agencies you've visited, and questioning teachers in brushup courses, you can say, "I'm told that the going rate for jobs like this one is $————." The fact that you are knowledgeable is a bonus in your favor.

Be specific, yet avoid pricing yourself out of the job.

If the interviewer asks, "What is the minimum you will take?" You might answer, "Before I can answer that, I'd like to know more what some of the benefits are and what additional training the firm gives to help one's advancement."

Don't forget that the Equal Pay Act of 1963 requires equal pay for equal work, regardless of sex.

9. If there is no opening in the job you have applied for, the way you present your qualifications may lead the interviewer to suggest a job in another department. Sometimes if the employer does not have any immediate openings, he may be impressed enough with you to suggest other firms that may have openings. I recall many times when I have done just that myself—because I had a favorable impression of the applicant and felt that she deserved a break. Should an interviewer make such a suggestion, be sure to jot down all the facts at once, checking the spelling when necessary or obtaining sources for further information. When you apply at the other firm, be sure you state who recommended you.

End of the Interview

Most interviews last about twenty to thirty minutes, not including the testing time. The interviewer will usually give you a clue as to when it is over. At that time, if the interviewer asks, "Do you have any questions?" it is in your favor if you can think of one or two to ask, especially if they show you know something about the firm. You might conclude by saying that you have been interested in hearing about the job and hope you can be considered for it (if you really mean it!). The interviewer may indicate when you may expect to hear whether the employer has a job for you.

Employers who want a more detailed application blank filled out before they hire you will give you this form to take home, complete, and mail back.

Be prompt in leaving. Thank the interviewer. You may write a word of thanks if you want to, but it is not necessary in most cases.

You may ask, "But what shall I say if they offer me a job the day I apply?" Most firms will want to check your references and tests before they do that. And you will surely want to think over job offers before you accept them. However, if the employer offers you a job on the spot, and if you are absolutely sure you want it, *take it.* (Perhaps by this time, you will have had enough interviews to decide.) But if you don't want to be committed then and there, ask if you may think about it and call the next day. You will not be thought less of for doing so.

How Fast We Forget!

After you leave the office, find some quiet place where you can make a few notes about the interview, because you simply will not remember everything unless you do. One firm I know used to have a little card on which were listed all the benefits. This was helpful to applicants, who could review the facts later on.

There have been some interesting studies made on forgetting. One often quoted is the "Law of Diminishing Impressions" as formulated and tested by the late Dr. Walter Dill Scott of North-western University, Evanston, Illinois. The study shows that after twenty-four hours twenty-five percent of the people forget an ad. After two days fifty percent forget, after four days eighty-four percent forget, and after seven days ninety-seven percent forget.

Since we learn most of what we know through our eyes, not our ears, you can see why applicants forget fast what they have heard in an interview.

If you are just one of numerous applicants, remember that it takes time to check references and go over tests. If you do not hear from the firm in a reasonable time, and if you really want the job, then write a brief note to say you're still interested. You have nothing to lose and you may get a favorable answer.

You may ask, "Do employers *really mean it* when they say they'll keep your application on file for future openings?" If they consider your qualifications such that they might later want to hire you, they will certainly keep you on file. If they see little likelihood that you would qualify for anything they have or might have, they will probably tell you.

If You Are Offered a Job

1. It is disheartening to any employer to go through the interview process, check references, and offer a job to someone only to have her reply, "I want to work but I must have the summer off." If this is one of your job conditions, don't wait until the last minute to bring it up.

2. The employer will state when he wants you to start work. You have undoubtedly given careful thought to the fact that you're going to have to sacrifice some free time you used to enjoy. Also, if your teeth need attention or you require new glasses, get all this done before you start soliciting job offers. *If you really want to work, be ready to go when the chance comes.*

3. It is against the law for an employer to ask for a photograph *before* you're hired, but after you're accepted many employers will want a small photograph and will specify their requirements.

4. Most companies require job candidates to pass a physical

examination after they are accepted, but before they can actually go on the payroll. The company will give you a slip to the company infirmary, where the nurse and doctor will give the physical at no cost to you.

Smaller companies, which do not have an infirmary, quite often send applicants to a doctor's office for the physicals. This is also at company expense.

What if, after all of your preparations, the filling of applications and going through one or more interviews and tests, you *do not get the job*? Precondition yourself—right now—that you may have to face this situation, and possibly more than once. But don't consider it a personal "failure." As often happens, it is as much a case of the job not being right for you as you not being right for the job.

Chapter 10

Don't Panic—
You Can Pass the Tests!

As in doing crossword puzzles, so it is with job tests—certain people find them fascinating and others prefer no part of them. While some women find it interesting, challenging, even exhilarating to take such tests, many become very nervous.

Since you can help yourself a great deal by anticipating what to expect, this chapter is designed to give you some clear ideas about how to prepare for tests. The sample test in the Appendix about civil service jobs (Chapter 7) will give you a typical test to practice on. You also benefit by recent court decisions about testing. For some years, the Equal Employment Opportunity Commission has examined how such methods are used in hiring.

An Important Supreme Court Decision

In March 1971 the Supreme Court disallowed the use of intelligence tests or the requirement of a high school diploma for employment when neither standard is shown to be related to successful job performance, or when they tend to disqualify nonwhites at a higher rate than whites.

As a result, employers have looked into their examining programs to be sure their personnel tests do not violate the government's nondiscrimination guidelines.

Some Helpful Hints from the State Employment Service About Tests

Why Take an Aptitude Test?

Aptitude tests can help you find out what you can learn to do best. You may have the aptitudes needed for many different jobs. Aptitude tests show you some of the jobs you could learn if you had the chance and interest to do them. How should you study for aptitude tests? You can't study directly for them but you can get ready to do your best on them. How? *By taking tests.* Almost any you can take will help you learn how to take others. Try taking quizzes you see in newspapers, magazines, books, or even school texts. Be sure to set time limits for yourself, if they are not already specified. By taking tests you learn more about how questions are phrased and how to answer them.

Your Physical Condition Is Important

If you are not well, or if you are half asleep, you can't do your best work on aptitude tests. Here are some tips about being ready:

1. Get the same amount of sleep you usually get. Don't stay up all night worrying about the test.

2. If you require glasses or hearing aid, be sure to wear them when you go to take the test.

3. If you have any physical problem that may lessen your abilities, be sure to inform the supervisor giving the test. If you are sick or in poor health, it is better to make plans to take the test some other time.

Your Attitude Makes a Difference

Although many people complain about being nervous when they have to face a test, remember that whenever something important happens you are naturally inclined to get a little nervous. Often this performs the useful function of making you more alert and keeping you on your toes.

Allow plenty of time to get to the test—especially if it is some distance away—and even be early so you can sit down and relax for a few minutes beforehand.

Test Supervisors Are There to Help You

It is common to feel that the persons giving the test are trying to give people a rough time. But they are really trying to familiarize you with what to do and how to go about it. *Ask questions if there is anything you don't understand.*

Don't be the silent type who hesitates to speak up and then muffs simple questions because of not knowing the procedures.

Some Rules to Know

Rule 1. Work as fast as you can.

Most aptitude tests have short time limits and multiple questions. To get your best score you must work as quickly as you can. Be aware that each part is made so long that you can't finish, but the more you do correctly the better your score will be.

If you waste time on one question, either by trying to puzzle out the right answer or by changing the answer many times, you can't get to questions that might be easier. Don't let the hard part of the test block you from continuing on to the easy parts.

Rule 2. Whenever you think you know the right answer, put it down.

Don't answer a question when you are doubtful about the answer. *Do* answer a question when you think you know the answer, even if you are not sure it is right.

Rule 3. Always follow directions.

Start working on the test as soon as you are told to start, but not before. Stop when you are told to stop. A good test score means that you followed directions and marked the right answers. A poor test score could mean that you just didn't follow directions.

With some tests you mark your answers in the test booklet, with others on a separate answer sheet. You may fill in a space shaped like one of these: $\bigcirc$, $=$, or $\|$. It really doesn't matter what the answer space is like as long you take time enough to *follow instructions.*

Rule 4. Don't give up.

Some tests are easy, others are hard. But *don't give up* just because a test has difficult questions. It's just as hard for the others!

A Further Word on Tests

In addition to these helpful hints suggested by a state employment service, I would add that if possible have someone at home time you on typing tests. It is better, of course, to take the timed typing tests in a class.

If you will be asked to take a spelling test, remember that most people could make higher scores if they had trained themselves to be more observant. Then you'll easily notice more of those misspelled words or mistakes in grammar.

In my interviews with thousands of mature women who returned to work, among other favorable things I noticed was the fact that they could spell far better than today's young people. When researchers of the American Council on Education asked entering freshmen of sixty-one colleges and universities their career choices recently, their replies included these incredible samples of spelling: *bussenius, sailsmen, sicology, archetict, denestry, augriculter, airanatics,* and *piolet.* One student said he was "undisided."

Some firms give an arithmetic test. On this, as well as on the typing and spelling, strive for *accuracy above speed.*

Business Has a Responsibility

Housewives tend to underrate their abilities.

While it is important for you to have built up your self-confidence, it is equally important for the employer in question to have the testing done by staff people who give the applicant the feeling that they *believe in the applicant's abilities.* A firm cannot expect to get good results in any test supervised by a person with an indifferent or unsympathetic attitude toward applicants.

Many tests are given on vocabulary and proficiency in using

words, since they are yardsticks that help to measure intelligence. Reading is one effective way to improve word power, and many magazines and newspapers have columns devoted to increasing one's vocabulary. Using such aids will help you.

John Barbour, Associated Press Newsfeatures writer, told of his childhood experience with tests. He said, "When I was in seventh grade my family moved to Detroit, where I was given an IQ test. My score was first-grade level. My homeroom teacher said, 'John, you have the best manners of anyone in school, but I wouldn't plan on going to college.' So, I approach intelligence tests with some dismay. I can see my homeroom teacher spinning around in her grave, and that awful blank on the test paper where I couldn't define an octagon. However, after talking to psychologists from Washington to Princeton, N.J., for an AP story on the elusive meaning of intelligence and its measure, I felt my inferiority complex melting away.

"Psychologists protest the misuse of tests. For instance, when a teacher tells a student with a low test score that he should change his plans for the future. Or worse, when the teacher gives up on the youngster in the classroom."

To sum up the whole matter of testing and taking tests, the best advice I can give is: Don't belittle yourself. If you score low in one type of test, it may well mean that you are striving too hard in an area where you are not proficient and overlooking another field where you could make out very well. By looking into many types of job areas—scattering your shots, in effect—you will eventually zero in on the target so that you can make the best score.

That is what testing is all about.

Chapter 11

Your Salary—Will It Satisfy Your Money Needs?

Considering and achieving the salary you want is only one step. You are inviting trouble if you don't first figure out how you will allocate and manage the income you will be getting.

If I tried to list typical salaries for various types of jobs, the information would be out of date even before this book came off the press. The *Occupational Outlook Handbook,* mentioned previously, can give you some idea, but since it is printed only every few years, many of the salaries mentioned in its pages are already out of date. Salaries vary greatly, too, from small town to big city, as well as in various regions of the country. They depend on many factors, including the skill and responsibility required for the work, the experience you bring to the job, and the location, size, and type of an employer's business.

You can get a fairly reliable idea of salaries through the sources I mentioned earlier, such as your own study of want ads, the experience of employment agencies, and listings with government employment services.

The Importance of Money Management

Because I've seen too often how the mismanagement of money can affect families adversely, how it affects getting and holding a job, let us consider some of these problems first. Perhaps you will take the outlook of one woman who said, "We finally got tired of being broke from payday to payday. When I decided to go back to work to help out, it was with the objective of pulling ourselves together, agreeing upon family goals, and telling our money where to go instead of wondering where it went."

Naturally, there are those who are convinced that all the problems would be solved if they just had more money. But financial counselors know that a family with a $60,000 annual income can be in just as much financial trouble as one with $6,000.

Misuse of Credit

A family financial crisis has sent many a wife back to work. In the past decade, buying on credit has zoomed. While there is no doubt that installment plans have been a boon to many families, credit misuse has caused all sorts of gloom—and doom.

Bankers, financial counselors, and social workers all agree that financial problems can undermine marriage. The Tracers Company of America has said that the number of husbands who have disappeared each year since 1950 has steadily increased. The average husband who skips out is between forty-four and fifty-one years of age, is in sales or has occupied a semiexecutive position, and has had some two and a half years of college. What is the main cause of triggering the takeoffs? Overextended credit.

Money problems can have disastrous effects on your ability to get and hold a job. Although the garnishment laws have been eased lately, it is still estimated that between 100,000 and 300,000 workers lose their jobs each year because of garnishments.

The number of bankruptcies has increased in recent years. According to the Institute of Life Insurance, "Studies of people in bankruptcies show that many of them are in financial straits because they have, over a long period of time, let relatively small debts accumulate until they were unmanageable."

Bankruptcy and having your salary garnisheed can mar an otherwise good employment record, sometimes for years to come.

As the late Will Rogers once said, "This would be a great world to dance in if we didn't have to pay the fiddler. First payments are what made us think we were prosperous, and the other nineteen are what showed us we were broke."

Where to Get Help

"Love, honor, and learn to budget" is a marriage vow a family service counselor wishes couples would take, especially when there are two incomes in the family. Many private organizations and economic groups, such as businesses, educators, churches, and consumer advisers, have established community workshops, clinics, and counseling services to help people avoid financial crisis. Quite a few primary and secondary schools and youth groups, using publications supplied by financial institutions, have established courses to teach young people money-management concepts.

Watch your local papers for announcements of such courses, commonly offered in the early fall and again in the spring. Many of them are free.

Here are some specific examples of what planned spending can accomplish for you, and where you can find instruction:

1. Erna K. Carmichael, consumer marketing agent, who arranges the "Success in Managing Your Money" classes sponsored by the Milwaukee County Extension Office, University of Wisconsin, talks about planned spending.

Each person in the course—which covers money, how to spend it, how to manage it, and what it costs to get it—has a chance to work out a personal, tailor-made budget with the teacher's help. Mrs. Carmichael finds—as do financial institutions—that just handing a person a budget book seldom gets results. What might work for one person will not work at all for another. It's like wearing another person's shoes.

In this course, which covers typical subjects, there are six weekly sessions of two hours each on these topics. Why People Spend Money, Your Food Dollar, Need for Record Keeping, Understanding Life Insurance, Credit vs. Cash, Cost of Transportation, Make Your Own Budget, and Cost of Housing.

The course, workbooks, and the bulletins are all free. Couples are urged to attend together, and quite a few do. Mrs. Carmichael reports that many of the couples have been married at least seven or eight years and that few young people show up. But all come with the feeling that they can do far more with their incomes by studying planned budgeting and spending.

This popular course is offered twice a year in a number of locations. Several of the teachers are housewives (home economists) who work part-time teaching the classes.

Similar courses are offered across the United States in the extension divisions of state universities and land-grant colleges. Write to the extension service of your state university to ask what educational material they have on planning financial security and where money-management classes are held.

2. In many cities there is a Family Service Association. I talked with a counselor at one FSA office who said people in all income brackets come for help. FSA charges moderate fees based on ability to pay. If a family cannot afford to pay, the fee is waived altogether.

One Family Service counselor has said, "The way people manage their money is the way they manage their personalities." For the name and address of the agency nearest you, write to Family Service Association of America, 44 East 23rd Street, New York, N.Y.

3. Many banks and other financial institutions have "budget books," some free and some at low cost, which are helpful in planning home finances, and many banks offer lectures on budgeting. Although it would be impossible to list all of them, you will find in the appendix of this book a list of helpful publications and sources of information on money management. Unfortunately, too many people wait until they have a financial crisis before they seek help.

4. The new Plan Ahead Center at the First National Bank of Chicago (one of the nation's largest) has attracted a good deal of attention. Harold D. Pletcher, vice-president, talked with me about the center, which opened in 1969, after his bank had made an extensive study of what other institutions were doing in this field.

The center, which offers a free service to persons at all income levels, reminds me of the kind of medical center that is established to prevent illness rather than seeking a cure after people get sick.

You can go there to get a "financial checkup", to find out what your money habits are doing to your financial health, and to learn how to take a new look at your spending habits. Here are some questions the center asks you:

Where's Your Money Going Now?
Where does the money go? Sudden medical bills . . . school clothes . . . a new lawn mower? A Plan Ahead Specialist will go over your everyday spending—item by item—to help you find out. He'll show you how to cut on needless spending, and then help you plan a budget so you can pay bills now—and save for the future!

What Are Your Future Needs?
COLLEGE . . . How will you finance your children's college education? A Plan Ahead Specialist will work with you to find the best way to prepare for your family's educational expenses. Our College Specialist is trained to help you find colleges best suited for your children and to answer your questions about tuition, scholarships, and entrance requirements.

BUYING A NEW HOME . . . The decision to buy a home is one of the biggest you'll ever make. Our Plan Ahead Specialists will show you how much you can comfortably afford to spend. They'll explain things like mortgages and supply you with a lot of other facts, too, like the price range of homes in the city or suburban areas in which you are interested, the taxes, the school systems, and other areas of concern.

RETIREMENT . . . Whatever you want for your retirement years— a new occupation, travel, maybe moving to a sunny resort—Plan Ahead Specialists will help you plan for it. What can you expect in the way of retirement income? Our Specialists will help you combine your available fixed income (social security, pensions, etc.) with additional income (insurance programs, savings, other investments) to help you find out. Then, so you can make the most of your retirement years, he'll assist you in working out the best investment plan for you.

What's the Best Way to Prepare? . . . There are lots of ways you can put your savings plans to work. A Plan Ahead Specialist can explain them all—the many kinds of savings accounts, the different types of insurance policies, and all the other ways of investing your money. To make the most of what you have to save, it's best to know the pros and cons of each type. Once you know what they can do for you, you can decide which type, or combination, fits your way of thinking . . . and saving.

Because this is a popular service, one needs to *make an appointment* with a Plan Ahead Specialist. One experienced woman who is a Plan Ahead Specialist reports that many who seek advice are working women. She says, "Earning money is only half the job of a working woman. Spending it wisely is equally important."

I have written at some length about this Plan Ahead Center because it focuses on the kind of information and advice you need. I hope this discussion will motivate you to take seriously the long view of a job: what it means to plan ahead, and what fringe benefits can mean to you and your family in deciding on a job.

5. Recently the federal government published a free booklet called "Consumer Product Information," listing free or low-cost booklets on many subjects to stretch your dollar. For example, there are eight booklets on budget, credit, and finance, such as "Be a Good Shopper," "A Guide to Budgeting for the Family," "What You Should Know About Truth in Lending," "When You Use Credit for the Family," and "Consumer Protection." Some of the booklets are printed in Spanish.

To obtain consumer product information, write to Consumer Product Information, Washington, D.C. 20407.

This is only one booklet published by "Uncle Sam's Bookstore" among approximately twenty-seven thousand different publications, in forty-seven categories, which you may obtain from the Superintendent of Documents. "How to Keep in Touch with Government Publications" is an informative leaflet available from Superintendent of Documents, U.S. Government Printing Office, Washington, D.C. 20402. It describes the forty-seven categories and the price lists.

6. Women's magazines have published service columns for some time, but in recent years many newspapers have also run similar columns, on "Sense with Dollars," "More for Your Money," "Before You Buy," "Money in Your Pocket," and "Your Dollar's Worth," just to name a few.

Psychology and Money

The mother who is head of a household has special problems. Mothers are inclined to overspend on children when they cannot be with them as much as they would like.

Financial counselors agree that it is never wise to use money as a reward or punishment. Indeed, teaching a child to manage money is one of the most important family problems people have. "Start teaching children about money when they are in kindergarten," one expert advises.

What Will It Cost You to Work?

Consider job related expenses that will affect your situation when you go back to work:

Taxes

A wife's earnings often puts the husband into a higher tax bracket. Will you take yourself as a tax deduction or will your husband? There will be federal and possibly state and city income taxes, as well as social security.

Lunch and Refreshments

Where and what you eat seems like a minor point, but it can be a factor in choosing an employer. Many firms have fine cafeterias where food is served at cost. (Lunch is free in a few firms.)

Many women who work but a few blocks away return home for lunch. "I like to get away for those few quiet moments," say some. Others prefer having lunch downtown. "I get a better balanced meal than I ever did at home," is a typical comment, "where I just opened the refrigerator door and ate standing up for a few minutes."

Businesses do not mind your bringing lunch, although some specify a lunchroom or other place for "brown bagging." Many discourage, or even forbid food in any but a designated location because of problems with insects and sanitation.

Since the coffee break is here to stay, this becomes an additional expense for you. Of course, you don't *have* to eat or drink anything when you take a break, but most people do.

Personal Grooming

Once you go back to work you'll probably spend more on your appearance. Yet this has many advantages. For one thing, this may give a lift to the whole family. I have seen countless women look years younger after they have returned to work, and with a new zest for life that you can't get out of bottles—of pills or anything else.

Clothing

This may or may not be an added cost. In some jobs, such as reception clerks, tellers, and hostesses, uniforms are furnished. But, realistically, uniforms seem to be supplied largely in positions where younger girls are placed. Most women report that they do need a few new clothes when they go back to work.

Office Contributions

There always seems to be one person in an office afflicted with "giftitis." Although companies emphasize that employees must never be pressured to contribute, busybody do-gooders sometimes think that *their* cause is more important than company policy. Employees have different budget problems, and it is often embarrassing to be asked repeatedly to contribute to gifts one cannot afford.

"The real limit," said one woman, "was the day I started to work. Someone came up and asked if I'd like to contribute to a farewell gift for the woman I was replacing. I'd never laid eyes on her before. Why should I give her a present?"

Many firms urge supervisors to keep an eye on possible abuses of collecting for gifts. One firm solved the problem by suggesting that employees circulate an envelope to members of the department with names on a sheet. Then each employee could either add money to the envelope or merely cross her name off. The names of the donors and the amount remain anonymous. Gifts so purchased were to be given in the name of the department, with no individuals listed.

Many large firms have a policy of sending—at company expense —flowers or a memorial when a death occurs in an employee's immediate family, a process that saves a good deal of collecting time and effort.

"What I get sick of," an older woman said, "is this constant passing the hat for the wedding or shower gift. Then eventually another go-round when the little mother-to-be departs—a farewell gift and maybe something for the baby thrown in. It's really too much!"

You are under no obligation to donate to anything, but your own judgment has to be the guide. Be glad if you work where the company has some rules about these matters.

Union Dues

Not as many offices are unionized as factories. But, since some are, you may have to add dues to your budget.

Dues for Employee Clubs and Educational Organizations

Membership is voluntary. Further details about educational organizations, particularly, are in a later chapter about courses you may take after you're on the payroll.

Transportation

How you plan getting to and from work could actually save your family money. For example, as one woman said, "We were a two-car family. When I went back to work, we sold the second car, and now I use public transportation since one car is enough for us on weekends."

Others have said, "I landed a job close to home. I walk to work. I've lost twenty pounds and feel much better. Not only that, but I can buy attractive clothes in a smaller size where I always seem to find better bargains. My husband says I look like a new woman.

Some of my friends who don't work have to go to reducing salons."

Have you thought seriously about *bicycling* to work? Not only are many more women riding bikes these days, but so are the children. The increasing popularity of bikes helps to solve the chauffeur problem for mothers. It saves wear and tear on the car, to say nothing of car-pooling mothers. "Biking is great," say many enthusiastic cyclists, "I've shed all those pounds I wanted to lose, and it costs me nothing to get to work."

Riding a bike in a big city may seem a bit terrifying, yet thousands of people are doing it. A Chicago newspaper published an article recently about Helene Stoffey, president of the Association of Bicycle Commuters in Chicago. "Fall and spring are the best times to ride your bike to work," advises Ms. Stoffey. Since the big city bicycle commuter has one major worry—where to park the bike downtown—the article showed a map of bicycle parking facilities in downtown Chicago. Fees at garages range from 50 cents to $2.00 a day. Parking is free to employees at many firms that provide racks, while others may charge nominal fees per month to park a bicycle in an inside garage.

Joining a car pool is another way to save transportation costs. Learn the details first:

a. Know the rules of the pool before you join.

b. Ask whether you will pay by the week, month, or per ride. Most participants pay by the month, and are not charged when on vacation or away for a long illness. "We always pay the driver, though, if we're sick for just a day or two."

c. Be aware that the charge generally includes not only gas and oil, but tolls, normal maintenance, and parking space.

d. Find out whether the same person drives each week, or whether the riders take turns.

e. Ask as tactfully as possible, whether there will be a hassle about having the radio on, and, if it is on, tuned to which station. Especially in the morning, some people can't stand having a radio on. Others would rather have the radio on than have to talk. Other points of friction sometimes develop over whether the car windows shall be open or shut and whether smoking is permitted.

f. Learn what people talk about en route. One car pool that

rode in harmony for years had an ironclad rule: no discussion of business!

g. Find out about routes and order of picking up and letting off. Don't argue with the driver about who is going to be picked up first. Pool members try to figure out the shortest routes. Some pools meet in a central location if all live nearby, but generally the driver picks up the riders.

h. Be sure you know the hours and are willing to *be on time.* There may be one rider in every pool who practically holds a stopwatch on the others. Try to get into a pool where everyone comes and goes at about the same time. (When you know that you will have to work late, you must notify the driver.) Car pools drop persons who are habitually late.

Fringe Benefits—The Hidden Bonus

Some women treat fringe benefits as though they were not very important. "Oh, my husband has all that," many will say. If I could, I'd like to sit down with every woman who reads this book and say, "Please, please don't overlook how valuable fringe benefits can be to the working woman and her family."

Since benefits are tax free, you could be farther ahead financially if you took a lower paying job to start with a large firm that offers many fringe benefits than if you took a job in a small office that offered fewer. It depends on the job *opportunity,* though. I would never recommend taking a dead-end job just to get benefits. For women who are heads of households the benefits can be crucial in helping them to meet unexpected financial problems.

"Variations in fringe benefits can spell the difference between prosperity and just making do, or making do and bankruptcy," Arthur Louis wrote in "What You Should Know About Fringe Benefits" recently in *New York* magazine.

A 1972 survey of eight thousand firms reports that the annual fringe benefits of the average employee totals $2,052. Twenty years ago this figure was only $450. And there has been an increase of 2 to 4 percent over the past two years in the value of fringe benefits.

Firms with fewer than fifty employees pay 14 to 15 percent of their payroll toward the annual "hidden paycheck." Larger firms, the survey reveals, pay up to 30 percent, and in some cases even more. Benefits have grown far beyond the usual ones. In addition to increased insurance coverage, paid holidays, vacation, disability, and pension coverage, there is more sick leave, company clinic aid, cafeteria and coffee services, employee tuition refunds, scholarship programs, uniforms, discounts on goods and services, special library availability, and recreational programs, to name some.

Why Basic Benefits Are Important to You and Your Family

The American parent is portrayed so often in magazines and on television as never being over thirty-four, that it is often difficult to get anyone, male or female, to be concerned about old age.

Women must find out about their retirement benefits. A woman who goes back to work may well be able to put enough years into a job to build an attractive retirement income for herself or to supplement her husband's resources. Unfortunately, some people find themselves without a pension because of mergers, business collapse, or failure to join a plan that is voluntary.

Private pension plans have been in existence for more than eighty-five years, but social security records show that only about 4 million retirees receive private benefits. This number is low because the big push for pensions did not come until after World War II.

Why Many Older Women Live Alone and in Poverty

One out of four persons over sixty-five lives in poverty today. And the most likely candidates are women, because they live longer than men; they earn less than men; and many have little but social security for support.

The Women's Bureau, U.S. Department of Labor, reports these facts:

Women who work at full-time jobs the year round earn, on the average only $3.00 for every $5.00 earned by similarly employed men.

The ratio varies slightly from year to year, but the gap is greater than it was 15 years ago. From 64 per cent in 1955, women's median wage or salary income as a proportion of men's fell to 61 per cent by 1959 and 1960 and since then has fluctuated between 58 and 60 per cent. Women's median earnings of $5,323 in 1970 were 59 per cent of the $8,966 received by men.

MEDIAN INCOME IN 1970 OF FULL-TIME YEAR-ROUND WORKERS,
BY SEX AND YEARS OF SCHOOL COMPLETED.
PERSONS 25 YEARS OF AGE AND OVER

Years of School Completed	Median Income		Women's Median Income as Percent of Men's
	Women	Men	
Elementary School:			
Less than 8 years ..	$3,798	$6,043	62.8
8 years	4,181	7,535	55.5
High School			
1–3 years	4,655	8,514	54.7
4 years	5,580	9,567	58.3
College			
1–3 years	6,604	11,183	59.1
4 years	8,156	13,264	61.5
5 years	9,581	14,747	65.0

These figures do not necessarily indicate that women are receiving unequal pay for equal work. For the most part, they reflect that women are more likely than men to be employed in low-skilled, low-paying jobs.

You no doubt will notice that the median income for a woman with a college degree is less than the median income for a man with less than a high school diploma, and that the median income for a woman with an advanced degree is just $14 more than a man with a high school diploma.

The number of elderly persons living either alone or away from their children has increased dramatically in the last eleven years, the Census Bureau reported in February 1972.

In 1960 there were 2.3 million women aged sixty-five and over living alone or away from their families. In 1971, the figures had increased to 4.2 million, a jump of 82.6 percent. There were 904,000 men aged sixty-five and over living alone or away from their children in 1960. This number increased to 1.2 million in 1971, a nearly 38 percent boost.

An article, "How You Lose Money by Being a Woman," in the January 1972 issue of *McCall's*, explains graphically why such a disproportionate number of women are forced to live in poverty when they are old. Go to your library and read this article—do get the facts.

Employed women should examine their retirement benefits, and if married they should learn the provisions of their husband's benefits. Social security and pension plans are often based on the assumption that most women are married and supported by husbands. This kind of thinking leaves out the millions of women who are heads of households!

Consider these social security statistics: In 1967 the average retired male worker received $92.50 per month in social security, but for women workers the allotment was only $71.90. More than half the retirees with benefit payments of less than $70.00 were women. On the average, the retirement benefit of women workers was 76 percent of the average amount for men. Naturally, all these figures are higher now, but the proportion hasn't changed, and inflation has taken a cruel toll of all the amounts.

Life Insurance

Although many firms provide free life insurance, the amount they give can vary considerably. "It never occurred to me that it was important that I have life insurance," said a woman whose family is dependent on her income.

Have you thought about how fast circumstances can change?

"For there is no one so assured of his honor; of his riches, health or life, but that he may be deprived of either or all at the very next hour or day to come." So wrote Sir Walter Raleigh, imprisoned for fifteen years in the Tower of London before the axe fell on his neck. Sir Walter had a long time to think about how fast his circumstances had changed.

We do things faster now, and we face sudden catastrophes. In 1970, for example, over fifty thousand persons died in automobile accidents, while over two million were injured. The Insurance Information Institute has projected that the total economic loss— nationwide—from auto accidents in 1971 will be a whopping $16.35 billion. This averages out to about $250 per family. The loss factors include wages, medical expenses, property damage, and the costs of servicing insurance, among others.

Hospital and Major Medical Insurance

Some features of medical coverage have changed for the better for women. Just a few years ago many policies did not cover a woman's spouse or children at all. Now they do—or should. Although the nominal charge for this type of insurance is sometimes slightly more if you include your family, it is always lower than you would pay for similar insurance on your own. With medical bills what they are today, no one can afford to overlook benefits that pay up to 80 percent of the expense. Some firms do not limit you to one major medical expense per year. For women heads of households this insurance is especially important, since it is conceivable that they might have two or more major medical costs in one year.

Maternity Benefits

You will probably see a number of changes in maternity benefits in the coming months and years. Already many firms have eased their policies on maternity leave—some because they want to, others because they have had to.

The office of Federal Contract Compliance of the Department of Labor has established these guidelines:

Women shall not be penalized in employment because of time away for childbearing. It is a justified leave of absence. Following childbirth and signifying their intent to return within a reasonable time, female employees shall be reinstated to their original jobs or to a position of like status and pay without loss of service credit.

Firms vary in what they call "reasonable time" to return, but recent court rulings have said that the decision of when a pregnant woman should stop working or start again is best left up to the woman and her doctor.

Do Women Work Just for Money?

A Labor Department study, based on a nationwide study of more than five thousand women aged thirty to forty-four, concluded that income is not the sole motive behind women who work.

"The majority of employed women would continue their jobs," says the report, "even if they had enough money to live comfortably without working."

The study covered women's behavior in the labor market, their attitudes toward the role of women, education, previous work experience, health considerations, family income, the ages of children and whether they still live at home, and the use of child-care services.

"These factors are measured against the kinds of jobs women have, their earnings and hours of work, their job satisfaction and the stability of their employment," the report added.

What are the personal satisfactions, other than good pay and attractive working conditions, that make a job worthwhile? Researchers are continuously trying to find the answer, but what is meaningful to one person in a job may not suit another employee in a similar type of work at all.

Sometimes applicants say to me, "Do you think this is the *right* job for me?" I would never presume to try to answer that question for them, and neither would any other job counselor. The best we can do, as professionals in the employment field, is to supply facts, suggest sources of information, and provide as much as we can about the pros and cons. In the end the decision must be up to *you*. But that decision will be a great deal easier if you approach it armed with facts.

Chapter 12

Your First Days on the Job

What do you remember about your very first day on the job?

"I looked at the others starting the same day," said one woman who was going back to work, "several cute little miniskirted things and a bright young man, just out of college. I felt like Methuselah until I found out that they were all just as nervous as I was."

"What helped me feel most at home," reported another, "was the fact that a sponsor in the department took me to lunch as the firm's guest. They gave me a bundle of books to read, but it was that individual friendly welcome that made me feel I belonged there."

"I remember I couldn't wait to get to the department to see the *people* I'd be working with," said a third woman. "It was hard to keep my mind on a film they showed about the company."

Don't be discouraged to learn, though, that the First Day is likely to be the day "Murphy's Law" operates—if anything can happen it will—like the unexpected run in your hose, a cold in the head, getting lost on the way to work, forgetting to bring necessary records. Whatever you do, be prepared for the unexpected and don't panic.

Although employers really want you to feel welcome, the way they go about accomplishing this varies considerably. Some companies do a fine job of orientation for new employees, yet there are too many that invite rapid turnover by the way they treat people the first day on the job.

Your introduction to the firm really began during your employ-

130

ment interview. You can judge from that, many times, what your first days on the job might be like. One woman said, "My introduction to this firm was being interviewed by an inexperienced young girl recently out of high school. She didn't know beans about personnel interviewing. I was astounded that a firm so well known in the state would put such a person at the front desk in the personnel department."

Let's hope you have better luck. Introducing a person to a firm and to a prospective new job is serious business, not something to be shunted off to the untrained or the indifferent.

A realistic orientation program will try to:

1. Create a favorable attitude. Most companies want new employees to feel that they have found an amenable place to work. If the orientation includes only the barest process of listing an employee on the payroll, with no further effort to make a person feel comfortable, the company leaves itself wide open to having first impressions originate with disgruntled employees who want to get in their gripes to a receptive ear as quickly as possible. Since no office is heaven, there are bound to be some disgruntled people around. They seem to enjoy giving a poor impression to new people.

"I'll never forget my first day on the job," commented one woman who went back to work in an office. "I had thought the company was a pretty good one until a brash young fellow came up to me and said, 'Well, I hope you're going to be able to stand working for Growly George.' As it turned out the boss was congenial to me, and if he growled at the brash young man he deserved it. It was he who was the troublemaker."

2. Establish a feeling of belonging. Many companies arrange for someone on the staff to take each new employee for lunch at company expense. This is an excellent personnel practice, far less costly than ads saying "We are the friendly XYZ Company." If its employees don't think the XYZ Company is all that friendly, their comments can sabotage the big "friendly ad" any day.

3. Remove fears which may hinder learning a new job. People really want to know what is expected of them. The orientation you get and your supervisor's informative talk should accomplish this. Yet, if you are told too much on the first day, you won't remember

half of it. Some firms swamp the bewildered new arrivals with so much detail that they feel overwhelmed. Therefore, many firms present information as instructions in several stages, with follow-up talks by the supervisor until the person is securely established.

What a Good Orientation Program Should Tell You

Whether you start in a small office or large, here are some of the matters you should be informed about during your first few days on the job:

Tax Withholding

You will be told that, by law, your firm is required to make certain deductions from your salary.
1. Federal income tax withholding
2. State income tax withholding (in many states)
3. City and local income tax withholding (in a few locations)
4. FICA (social security)

Pay Day

You will quickly learn how often you are to be paid and on what days. Many firms pay every two weeks. Be sure you understand at the start what your exact rate will be. Many companies now use the checkless payroll, where your pay is deposited in a bank checking account. Your employer will tell you about this, and your earnings statement, which will show all the deductions, checks written, and other information.

Many banks provide free checking accounts for their employees, although in some you have to be on the payroll three months before your account is opened.

Insurance

Many firms provide free life insurance, the amount varying widely from one company to another.

Health insurance, hospitalization, and major medical insurance plans—both for individuals and families—are available in many offices. The employer usually makes a nominal charge for this, and will give you a booklet explaining the medical insurance plan, coverage, amounts paid for various illnesses or surgery, and other details. Again, the amount of coverage varies from company to company.

Retirement Plan

If there is a pension plan, employees will be able to obtain a copy of the plan that explains the eligibility rules, how the benefits are figured, who manages the funds.

Union Membership

Some offices are unionized, although not everyone is eligible to join. If you are, you will be informed how and when you can join. In some offices you can become a member right away, in others you may need to work three months or so, before being eligible. The conditions may vary, but when you do join you must be given a copy of the union contract.

Vacations

You will learn how soon you are eligible for a vacation, how long it will be, when you may take it, and how the length increases with your years of uninterrupted service.

Holidays

The number of paid holidays varies with each company, although generally the number has increased in recent years. In addition, some firms now give an extra day—either Friday or Monday—if a regular holiday such as the Fourth of July falls on a Saturday or Sunday, when the office is closed.

Some employers offer a "floating" holiday, which you may take at the convenience of your department. Some people like to lengthen their vacation with their floating holiday. Others use it for a long weekend, or for a special day.

Leaves of Absence

Leaves range from those for military service to those for maternity. As mentioned earlier, maternity leave varies. Although not long ago many firms gave leaves only in emergencies, this situation is changing.

Sick Leave

In many offices, you should not expect any paid sick leave until you've been on the payroll for a few months—three months seems to be a common probationary period.

Some offices allow an average of one day a month, which may not be carried over from year to year. A more beneficial plan is the cumulative sick leave, which does not have this calendar restriction. A generous sick leave plan is one in which employees are entitled to one-half day of sick leave for each month of service for the first four years on the job. Thereafter, the employees receive two and a half days of sick leave per month. This is cumulative to a maximum of 261 working days, or one full working year.

In any office, a record of frequent absences may lead to dismissal, because this creates a burden for the firm and for fellow employees who must make up for the lost manpower.

Training Programs

You may be starting a job that stipulates attendance at a company-sponsored class for training. If so, your department manager will tell you where to report, how long the class will take, and other details.

Tuition Refunds

Many firms refund whole or partial tuition for courses employees take that are related to business. A later chapter will describe where such courses may be found, and what they include.

Employee Clubs

In the larger firms there are usually one or more clubs—for athletic, social, and other recreational activities. Membership is voluntary and fees—if any—are small, usually to help pay costs of equipment or refreshments.

Job Posting

In unionized offices, jobs covered by the union are posted on the union bulletin boards when there are openings in various classifications. Some offices that are not unionized post job openings, too. Chapter 13 provides more information about this.

Salary Administration

After joining a firm—though usually at a later date—you will be informed about salary reviews and when you can expect your first pay raise. Some such raises are based on merit, others are on the cost of living. You will also learn how job performance is rated and what you can do to improve your own rating.

Suggestion Plans

Many firms have suggestion boxes or other means of obtaining suggestions and criticisms from employees.

Discounts on Products or Services

If you are going to work for a firm that manufactures consumer products or provides consumer services, you will probably be eligible, after a period of time, for discounts on these for you and for your family. Such benefits will vary with the firm in question.

Telephone Usage

Many firms give new employees booklets or fact sheets about correct telephone usage. It is very important that you learn at the start all the details about use of telephones (and other means of

communication) for business purposes. And be sure that you know
company policies regarding *personal* telephone calls. The misuse
of personal calls has caused headaches for many a company and
its employees.

Employee Manuals

Some firms furnish published manuals, while others feel that
just giving a person a bundle of books is a poor guarantee that the
employee has all the information needed or will even take the
trouble to read the material.

One personnel manager said, "Keeping employees posted about
company-provided benefits is one of the biggest personnel problems
we have." Another said, "The busy executive can be just as ignorant
about these matters as the lowest-paid person on the payroll." A
study by *Personnel* magazine showed that only 60 percent of the
white-collar employees surveyed at one company "had more than
an inkling of their major benefits."

The problem is *how* to get people to read and remember what
they should know about company policies and their own benefits.

A major oil company reported that employees aboard their
tankers are the most interested in fringe benefits because apparently
when they are at sea they have *plenty of time* to study literature
handed out.

The Supervisor's Responsibilities in Orientation

Many firms feel that the best road to employee orientation is to
be sure that the supervisor follows up regularly to be sure people
know both what is expected of them and what is coming to them.
Many review the highlights of the orientation at the end of the new
employee's probationary period. From time to time, too, firms issue
bulletins to announce changes in benefits. The responsible supervisor makes sure that employees read and understand such changes.

Often the personnel department undertakes general orientation
while the supervisor gets down to the individual and the specifics.
An office manager or supervisor who is properly qualified will inform you about:

1. Your job description
2. The objectives of the department
3. The relation of your role to the rest of the department
4. Standards of performance
5. Telephone usage in the department
6. Hours to be worked
7. On-the-job training
8. Lunch hour and work breaks
9. Time sheets—necessary for computing salary and overtime
10. When and whom to call, and what to report, if you are going to be unexpectedly absent or late for work
11. Other department regulations
12. Use of company infirmary, if there is one
13. How to report accidents or injuries on the job

Usually the supervisor will delegate a sponsor to stay with you during the first few days, to take you around the department, to introduce you to your fellow workers, to show you the rest rooms, locker space, time clock (if applicable), as well as to allocate your desk or work space.

You may say, "Well, I had a job once, and no one did any of these things—taking me to lunch, providing tours, introducing me around, and all that! They just plunked me down at a desk and said, 'If you have any questions, call me.'" Fortunately, the day is passing when a supervisor would snap, "I don't have time to bother with all this flapdoodle about getting new employees acquainted. We have work to get out. I'm busy!"

In many firms today supervisors are rated on their ability to develop and motivate the persons working under their direction. Management spends a great deal of money training supervisors and is well aware that turnover is costly. Nothing is more aggravating to a personnel department than to spend a good deal of time and money recruiting and hiring qualified employees, only to have them quit because of poor supervision!

If you have serious questions during your first days, ask your supervisor rather than the person next to you, who may have been there only a short time or who may be equally confused about policies and responsibilities.

If you are older and are worried about your relationships in working with young people, perhaps the experience of other women may reassure you.

"The kids really went out of their way to help me," many women report. This is true not only in job situations but when mature women have gone back to school or college, as you'll find out in Chapter 16.

"You just can't judge people by lumping them all together in one group. Take them one by one is the best advice I ever had in getting along with the people I work with."

"I spent quite a few years not talking to anyone much but children in the daytime. When I went back to work, it was so much fun to talk with adults during the day I didn't care whether they were eighteen or eighty!"

Your first job when going back to work may require *less than you are capable of doing*. Yet don't look upon it as a dead-end job, because you certainly are not a dead-end person! Think of yourself as an important human being, taking one step forward into a rewarding future.

I have seen many women who have returned to work in routine jobs who have been alert to the opportunities for training and advancement and who have progressed to high-ranking positions.

Moreover, there is a new government regulation—Revised Order 4—which may help you and many, many other women. Read on to see what Revised Order 4 means. April 3, 1972—the date on which this regulation became effective—may well be a landmark for women!

Chapter 13

Opportunity for Advancement

"Revised Order 4" may sound more like something out of a military document than a piece of legislation that might be beneficial to your interests. Yet right now it could help your return to work more than you could possibly imagine, and for the future it could change the entire attitude of business toward women. Let me explain this in a practical way and I'm sure you will see what I am driving at.

The woman who returns to work not only doesn't know a great deal about salary levels and benefits, but generally is little aware of the labor laws that affect her.

To understand Revised Order 4, we'll have to review a bit of labor history.

Title VII

On July 2, 1964, Congress passed the Civil Rights Act of 1964. Title VII of this act, "Equal Employment Opportunity," prohibits discrimination because of race, color, religion, sex, or national origin in hiring, upgrading, and all other conditions of employment. It became effective July 2, 1965.

Title VII established the Equal Employment Opportunity Commission, composed of five members appointed by the President and confirmed by the Senate.

Era of Tokenism

Then followed a false-front approach to a massive problem. Many employers put "We Are an Equal Opportunity Employer" in their ads and tried to hire some minority workers. But as the minorities pointed out, "They'd hire one, seat him in a conspicuous place near the door, and shout, 'See, we've got one.' " This is what blacks call the "showcase black."

Some employers said, "We'd really like to hire more minority people, but few ever apply; or if they do, they are not qualified." After years of being rejected, it should have come as no surprise that there was not a huge pool of highly trained minority workers.

Executive Order 11246

To help minorities become qualified and find jobs, former President Johnson issued Executive Order 11246 to all federal contractors to prepare a plan to end discrimination. This required getting minority workers into all areas of a business. Employers could no longer use the excuse, "No minority job seekers ever apply." They had to get out and *look for* minorities and then take steps to help them become qualified through various training plans. Just hiring a minority worker was no longer enough of an action to qualify a firm as an "equal opportunity employer." Now management had to be concerned with the upward mobility of the minorities and work with the U.S. Department of Labor, Federal Contract Compliance Office, to make sure they met the requirements.

What About Women in This Action?

Women seem to have been forgotten, even though Title VII said they were not to be discriminated against. Therefore, the Women's Bureau and various women's groups brought pressure to ensure that women would be included in a federal contractor's affirmative action plans for hiring and upgrading. Finally, Executive Order 11246 was revised to include women.

What Does This Mean?

On August 26, 1971, the United States Department of Labor made an announcement. It said in part:

A proposal for significantly improving the employment opportunities for American women was announced by Secretary of Labor J. D. Hodgson.

Regulations specifying "affirmative action" requirements among Federal contractors in all industries, other than construction, have been newly revised to include women.

Known as Revised Order 4, the regulations will require Federal contractors and subcontractors to develop goals and timetables to "remedy underutilization of women," Secretary Hodgson said. He expressed confidence that, when effective, this revised regulation "will have a great impact on our efforts to assure women equality in the American workplace."

"By providing well-defined criteria for correcting underutilization of women, this order will insure significant new job opportunities for American Women," Mr. Hodgson added.

Revised Order 4 became effective April 3, 1972.

Who Is a Federal Contractor?

Just about any business you can name holds federal contracts. Among the sixty-three types that do are insurance companies; utilities; real estate firms; printers and publishers; medical, legal, and educational services; schools, colleges, and universities; wholesalers and retailers; communication companies; motion picture producers; and banks. How, you might ask, could a bank be a federal "contractor?" Like most people, you are probably thinking of a contractor as a firm that supplies trucks, builds military planes, or engineers highways. Yet, since about twelve thousand of the fourteen thousand commercial banks in the United States have federal deposits, they are considered contractors.

The list includes all the businesses where women are employed in great numbers. All federal contractors who employ more than fifty persons and have federal contracts for more than $50,000 must now file affirmative-action statements with goals and time-tables for meeting Federal Contract Compliance rules on equal employment of women. They must keep separate lists of the minorities and women to avoid counting anyone twice—as for example, a black woman.

What Must the Companies Do?

To get more information about details, I talked with two defense compliance review specialists, Charlotte Higbee, a lawyer, and Janet E. Crosby, a former teacher. Both women have a substantial background in the Equal Rights Division of the state's Department of Industry, Labor, and Human Relations. As a black woman, Mrs. Crosby wears two hats, one for blacks and one for women.

A compliance review specialist calls upon the contractors to check out the equal opportunity programs and to offer technical assistance. "We are now hearing the same things we heard about blacks," said Mrs. Crosby, speaking of women, "that women don't apply for jobs, that they are not qualified, that they lack the needed skills."

The requirement that employers tell women about employment policies is very important to women. If they don't know what is going on, the contractor is not living up to his obligation. More-over, women will stay clustered in the lowest paid jobs if they are not aware of the opportunities which might be theirs with proper preparation.

Mrs. Crosby gave me a sample of a typical statement of policy:

It has been and shall continue to be the policy of (NAME OF OPERATION AND CORPORATION) that there shall be no dis-crimination based on race, sex, age, color, religion, or national origin in any personnel activity or action including recruiting, selection, hiring, placement, formal and informal training (such as On-the-Job-Training, Co-op Programs, Apprenticeships, and Management Training Pro-grams), seniority listings, transfers, promotions, layoff, recall and termi-nation.

Similarly, all salaries, wages, insurance programs and social and recreational programs will be administered in conformity with this policy.

Responsibility for maintaining an audit and preparing reports relating to our Equal Employment Opportunity and Affirmative Action Programs is assigned to (Name and Title) who will report to me each month with regard to progress and problem areas.

My personal commitment to this policy is complete. It is my deliberate intention that my actions and decisions will support the spirit of this policy and program. It is incumbent upon every employee to do the same.

_____

Signature and Title of the Highest Official

Revised Order 4 states that the federal contractor is to disseminate his policy internally as follows:

1. Include it in the contractor's policy manual

2. Publicize it in the company newspaper, magazine, annual report, and other media

3. Conduct special meetings with executives, management, and supervisory personnel to explain the intent of the policy and individual responsibility for effective implementation

4. Schedule special meetings with all other employees to discuss policy and explain individual employee responsibilities

5. Discuss the policy thoroughly in both employee orientation and management training programs

6. Meet with union officials to inform them of policy and to request their cooperation

7. Include nondiscrimination clauses in all union agreements, and review all contractual provisions to ensure they are not discriminatory

8. Publish articles covering Equal Opportunity programs, progress reports, and promotions of minority and female employees in company publications

9. *Post the policy on company bulletin boards.* I emphasize this point, because many firms are not big enough to have a company publication

10. Depict both minority people and women when employees

are featured in advertising, employee handbooks, or similar publications

11. Communicate to employees the existence of the contractor's affirmative action program and make available such elements of this program as will enable such employees to know of, and avail themselves of, its benefits

How Do Federal Contractors Put Their Policies into Practice?

1. They prepare a "skills" inventory first to find out what training is needed to bring women and minorities into the program.

2. They re-evaluate their selection methods and procedures.

3. They set training and long-range goals.

4. Federal contractors are given definite time limits to accomplish the various goals.

What Revised Order 4 Has to Say About Promotion

The contractor should insure that minority and female employees are given equal opportunity for promotion and other advancement. Suggestions for achieving this result include:

1. Posting or otherwise announcing promotional opportunities.

2. Making an inventory of current minority and female employees to determine academic, skill, and experience level of individual employees.

3. Initiating necessary remedial, job training, and work-study programs.

4. Developing and implementing formal employee evaluation programs.

5. Making certain "worker specifications" have been validated on job performance-related criteria. (*Neither minority nor female employees should be required to possess higher qualifications than those of the lowest qualified incumbent.*)

You cannot expect all blacks to be "superblack" or women to be "superwomen" before you will promote them! As a woman lawyer spokeswoman for the National Organization for Women said, "We won't be satisfied until an average woman can go as far as an average man."

6. Requiring supervisory personnel to submit written justification whenever apparently qualified minority or female employees are passed over for upgrading.

As one woman said, "Maybe this will help eliminate some of the managers who refuse to promote women or blacks simply because they are so prejudiced against them."

Elizabeth Duncan Koontz, Deputy Assistant Secretary of Labor and Director of the Women's Bureau, says on this topic: "We all know some people with incisive minds and great perception who really go 'up the wall' when you start talking about sex discrimination. Their own cultural biases, their own conditioning, get in the way.

"I would predict that the company that has this kind of person and this kind of staff will be left behind in the decade ahead. The narrow-minded person who is so biased that he cannot re-evaluate his old opinions and ideas will hold the company back. Why? Because business is going to have pressure from those who have the legal responsibility for removing this kind of injustice."

Many progressive firms today rate their supervisors and managers on their ability to develop the best potentials of the persons who work for them.

7. Establishing formal career counseling programs to include attitude development, education aid, job rotation, and similar programs.

8. Reviewing seniority practices and seniority clauses in union contracts to ensure that they are nondiscriminatory and do not have a discriminatory effect.

Mrs. Higbee and Mrs. Crosby said that in some firms well-trained supervisors brought back details of the company's affirmative action plans for women. In others the company preferred the women to get detailed information from the personnel department. But in any event, both women stressed—and I add my urging—*women should ask about the programs!* Don't just sit back. Find out what your options are, and be prepared to do your part to train for them.

What Federal Contractors May Not Do

1. Make distinctions, based on sex, in job opportunities, wages, hours, or other employment conditions.

2. Advertise for workers in newspapers under Male or Female unless that's a legitimate qualification.

3. Make distinctions for married or unmarried women, unless the same distinctions are made for men.

4. Penalize women who require time away from work for childbearing, which must be considered a justification for leave of absence for a reasonable time.

5. Maintain seniority lists based on sex.

6. Restrict one sex to certain job classifications and departments, and specify sex differences in either mandatory or optional retirement.

7. Deny a female any job she's qualified for under the excuse of a state protective law.

There is much more to Revised Order 4. I've tried giving you some of the highlights that you should know about. I urge you to get your own copy of Revised Order 4. Write to U.S. Department of Labor, Office of Federal Contract Compliance, Washington, D.C. 20212.

What Happens If a Federal Contractor Does Not Comply?

If a federal contractor does not meet the legal requirements or does not attempt to meet his goals and timetables, the compliance specialists told me, "The Office of Federal Compliance does not apply sanctions right away. We attempt to negotiate and conciliate and often in this way improvements are made."

If a federal contractor still fails to meet the requirements he could lose his contract.

For example, the Women's Equity Action League (WEAL), a group whose membership includes many women lawyers and a number of congresswomen, filed charges against one hundred colleges and universities claiming noncompliance with the executive

order forbidding discrimination. Now the government is withholding, or threatening to withhold, funds from several universities
until they put into effect the affirmative action equal employment
program to increase the number of minority members and women
in faculty staff positions.

Business Prepares for Changes

To observe the impact on business, I recently attended a conference in Chicago sponsored by the Urban Research Corporation
in cooperation with the International Business Machines Corporation, Cummins Engine Company, Inc., Illinois Bell Telephone
Company, Sears, Roebuck and Company, and the First National
Bank of Chicago. There more than six hundred top business, industry, labor, and government leaders met to discuss equal opportunity for women and the impact of Revised Order 4.

Forty top government officials, including William H. Brown
III, head of the Equal Employment Opportunity Commission in
Washington, D.C., corporate executives, and feminists spoke on
what is required by law, what is advocated by women's groups,
and what corporate programs are already in place.

Rights Movement No Laughing Matter at
Revised Order 4 Conference

There are those whose only grasp of the women's movement
seems to be what they have hastily glimpsed on a late night talk
show. Such persons seem to think that the whole movement con-
sists of "a bunch of crazies who go around burnings bras."

A leading conference participant suggested that the bra myth be
buried at once. This has been a favorite device of the media to
trivialize the women's movement, but bras have *nothing whatever*
to do with gaining equal pay and opportunity for women.

The *Wall Street Journal* later wrote, "If the women's liberation
movement was once treated as a major joke in the boardrooms of
corporate America—as most women say it was—the laughter now
is ringing hollow. Companies across the country now are finding

that they're going to have to come to grips quickly with demands for women's equality on pain of substantial financial penalties."

A conference participant, Jan Blakslee of the Cummins Engine Company, Inc. (one of the sponsors of this meeting), summed it up when he said, "If management can read the tea leaves, they're going to have to develop pro-active stances toward women. For one thing, it's going to cost them a bundle if they don't."

A Figure to Remember—the 96 Percent

Conference participants were well aware that women have reason to complain about equal pay and opportunity. Let me illustrate.

According to an article by John Kenneth Galbraith, Edwin Kuh, and Lester C. Thurow in the August 22, 1971, issue of the *New York Times* magazine, "In the better salary brackets of the business corporations, women, Blacks, Spanish-speaking citizens, and American Indians have only token representation. For all practical purposes, jobs here are monopolized by white males. The figures are uncompromising. In 1969, white males accounted for only 52 percent of all wage and salary earners in private and public employment, but they had 96 percent of the jobs paying more than $15,000 a year. Women make up about 30 percent of the full-time labor force. Only 2 percent of the women so employed had incomes over $15,000."

Mrs. Aileen Hernandez spoke about this problem at the conference. Mrs. Hernandez was one of the five commissioners appointed by the President and approved by the Senate, when Title VII established the Equal Employment Opportunity Commission. She is a past president of the National Organization for Women, presently heads its advisory board, and has her own consulting firm in San Francisco.

"Part of the problem," said Mrs. Hernandez, "is a sense of insecurity of white men at the top. They are getting frightened now because there is a whole new pool of resources—women, blacks, Chicanos—who do not want to divide up the small piece of pie that is left for them. They want to bake a whole new pie."

"White males need to develop a sense of security. They will

have to get over the idea that just being white and male will give a sense of security. We will need to make this a society where all individuals count. An individual should be judged on competence to do a job, not on sex or color."

Gloria Steinem, prominent spokeswoman on equal rights for women, pointed out how the press has trivialized and minimized the women's movement. She feels that an example of the women's struggle has been the difficulty of getting accurate coverage in the press of the women's movement activities.

One of the government officials at the meeting stressed making an inventory of the women already on the staff. "Identify them and their background. Find out what their aspirations are." Pointing out that many firms have college graduates working as secretaries, he added, "Get the women out of the clerical staff jobs into the training programs and professional jobs. We have brainwashed a lot of people into thinking they'll never be considered for these jobs.

"In many companies management trainee programs are one of the ladders to management positions. Traditionally, few, if any, women have been admitted into these programs. An important element of affirmative action shall be a commitment to include women candidates in such programs."

Management Awareness

Spokesmen for some of the companies with nationwide offices explained at this conference what they are doing.

Ray J. Graham, director of equal opportunity, Sears, Roebuck and Company, with thirty thousand employees (51 percent are women) spoke about their program. They have surveyed their full-time women workers and have found "many more than we would have guessed" who are promotable two steps beyond where they now stand. "We are identifying them and their career aims, long range ambitions, attitudes toward possible relocation. We intend to expand, rather than replace, which we can do, fortunately, because our business is an expanding one. The affirmative action program is one I heartily approve of. Business management has come to realize that the women's movement is a serious matter and must be dealt with in the same way as other matters. Now companies will be able to capitalize on the abilities and potential of all their employees. Sears is taking gender out of all job titles."

For those women who have gone back to work and settled for low-ranking jobs, even though they are capable of doing better, it should be encouraging to cite Mr. Graham's conviction that it is much more efficient for a company to promote from within than to hire from the outside. Sears has found it much less costly to develop management training programs for its own employees than to search nationwide for someone already trained.

There are always some firms, though, which will continue to search for the "superblack" and the "superwoman," rather than trying to promote their own.

John M. Clark, vice-president of the First National Bank of Chicago said, "We plan to utilize currently employed women, determine their capabilities, and give them the same shot at better jobs as male counterparts. We have many talented women who have not been considered or encouraged to push themselves forward for promotional opportunities because of stereotyped roles. We intend to improve their representation in management positions."

Louis M. Porter, Midwest employment manager for the Xerox Corporation, said that a study of the three thousand employees in his charge showed eighty-five women with college degrees being used largely in clerical jobs. "They had a lot more ability than that, and many had higher career goals."

Many participants at the Chicago meeting felt that secretaries long known as the "right arm" of top executives should be, and could be, moved to higher-ranking jobs.

Susan Davis, vice-president of the Urban Research Corporation, which sponsored the conference, said that industry surveys showed that managers generally had more promotable women than they expected to find and that they knew more about their men employees than their women.

Ms. Davis feels very strongly that housewives are never given credit for what they know and that this "invisible experience" is not taken into account when a woman goes back to work. Ms. Davis said, "The housewife is rebuffed and told she has no skills when actually she has had maybe at least ten years' experience in total home production."

And I take issue with those managers who say, "Oh, you know women are too emotional. They can't stand pressure." Do they ever try to visualize the woman who copes with the front door and the back door bells ringing at the same time while she is on the telephone, and while one tot has just dumped Mother's box of face powder down the toilet and another is fixing to pull something off the stove? *Who* can't cope with pressure?

How to Change Long-Held Corporate Attitudes Toward Women

In addition to preparing affirmative action plans, a number of companies have been grappling with trying to change long-held corporate attitudes toward women. It's one thing to enact a labor law, but quite another to get full cooperation through a change in attitudes.

Barbara Boyle, assistant manager of the IBM Corporation, described in detail the program her company has used for more than a year and a half, putting it well ahead of many firms in its affirmative action plans for women.

This firm requires all of its managers to take part in a three-hour program on sex bias, including a $50,000 film for managerial viewing on problems that confront workers. The half-hour film is entitled "The 51%" (the number of women employed).

IBM feels that it is important to have an educational program to bring out the prejudices. "You have to understand attitudes to change them," Miss Boyle said. She stressed the fact that IBM was not trying to create "showcase women," but to give many women a chance to progress.

After its managers have had this "awareness" training, the firm wants each manager to sit down with each one of the women in his department and talk about the next two jobs and what it takes to get there. The manager finds out what each woman's goals are, as well as her commitments, and encourages her to do some investigating herself.

Encourage women to set goals for themselves "because it's good business to do this," said Miss Boyle. She feels that unless you have realistic targets and objectives, nothing will happen.

What About Hostility Toward Women?

A conference participant from the Proctor & Gamble Company of Cincinnati, Ohio, said that women often have a low self-image. This outlook, along with the low image some men have of women, has weakened the aspirations of women for top jobs. When these things change, said the speaker, women could move easily into management positions. "That won't happen by hiring a woman vice-president, but by channeling women into the system so they can rise within it." When asked if he foresaw hostility, he replied that he did, but that "most of it will come from men who are insecure."

All of us who have worked have found that most of the hostility and failure to give women better opportunities have come from *insecure* people, whether they are male or female.

Skepticism About Revised Order 4

Some of the black personnel officers (male) at this meeting were skeptical about how well Revised Order 4 will work, because they felt some employers have not met their requirements about affirmative action plans for minorities.

Aileen Hernandez, a black woman, did not share their pessimism. "Women have a great deal of staying power," she said, "and we intend to make Revised Order 4 work." She did not feel Revised Order 4 would dilute the original order for minorities.

John Naisbitt, president of the Urban Research Corporation, which has sponsored these conferences in various sections of the country, is an optimist, too. Says Mr. Naisbitt, "Too many executives see this as a compliance problem, instead of seeing it as an opportunity to draw from this extraordinarily talented labor pool."

Beyond this conference, there is action elsewhere to improve opportunities for women.

How the State Employment Services Will Help Employers Implement Revised Order 4

I have talked several times with Mary Bresnahan of the Wisconsin State Employment Service, Madison, Wisconsin. She understands your problems very well, since she herself returned to work after being widowed. A graduate of the University of Iowa with extensive experience in public relations and social work, her job is to work with business, labor, government, industry, and community organizations to promote equal opportunity for women.

Some of her main concerns are to reach the woman who wishes to re-enter the labor market and to affect employment and promotion practices at the local state employment services.

In 1971 the Women's Bureau issued a pamphlet, *A Guide to Conducting a Consultation on Women's Employment with Employers and Union Representatives,* and has held demonstration projects in Atlanta, Boise, Boston, Detroit, and Kansas City, Missouri. Mrs. Bresnahan said that the various state employment services expect to use this booklet to arrange similar business-industry-union consultations.

You might like to see this booklet yourself. Ask for Pamphlet 12, *A Guide to Conducting a Consultation on Women's Employment with Employers and Union Representatives,* U.S. Department of Labor, Employment Standards Administration, Women's Bureau, Washington, D.C. 20210.

A number of conference participants at the Chicago meeting were concerned about the *availability* of women. The state employment services stand ready to help employers, in many ways, including application of the statistical studies they make. Late in 1971, I talked with Glenn O. Gronseth, research analyst in the Minnesota Department of Manpower Services, who told me about the various statistical studies available to employers. These included an analysis of the Duluth Active Application File according to experienced and inexperienced workers and veterans in separate files. The study listed occupational titles, age groups, total number of applications, breakdown according to sex and education.

I mention these things to stress again that it pays to register at the State Employment Service.

New York City Sets Precedent On Affirmative Action

The January 1, 1972, issue of *The Spokeswoman* said:

In a landmark precedent, New York City has issued rules requiring affirmative action for women among companies doing business with the city. Failure to implement these affirmative action plans could mean cancellation of contracts, withholding of payments or disqualification from bidding on work for the city. The guidelines require companies to specify salary discrepancies, benefits, promotions and job opportunities and to present plans for equalization.

Specifically contractors must:

1. Open all jobs to men and women and remove sex-based restrictive titles from job descriptions.

2. Base qualifications for positions on ability or performance, with testing being strictly objective and job-oriented.

3. Develop goals and timetables for the employment, upgrading and recruitment of women to correct existing deficiencies.

4. Add the tag "men-women" after the phrase "equal opportunity employer" in advertisements. Contractors are to avoid depicting women solely as docile, ever-cleaning housewives or sex objects.

5. Give women the same compensation as men performing the same jobs as well as equal pension, vacation and sick leave benefits.

6. Assure women of an opportunity to participate in all company training programs.

7. Eliminate from employment application forms questions about marital or parental status.

8. Grant maternity leave without fixed dates and assure a position upon the woman's return.

Thousands of companies will be affected. For example, the purchasing department reportedly has contracts valued at $150-million with 7,000 concerns for materials and supplies. The new guidelines will be enforced by the Office of Contract Compliance.

The above is from *The Spokeswoman,* an independent monthly newsletter of women's news, which also runs Help Wanted ads.

Susan Davis, vice-president of the Urban Research Corporation is its editor and publisher.

Anyone may use material from the newsletter as long as *The Spokeswoman* (including name, address, and cost) is credited. Subscription price is $7 per year by individual check, $12 per year by institutional check, 5464 South Shore Drive, Chicago, Ill. 60615.

Equal Opportunity Is a Two-Way Street

"Don't forget to remind the women that equal opportunity is a two-way street," says Mrs. Crosby, one of the federal compliance specialists. "With it comes *equal responsibility*."

You will have to help yourself, too. In the next chapter you will learn some ways you can do this after you are back at work and have a chance to consider the many courses that forward-looking companies offer.

Chapter 14

How to Help
Yourself Advance

Our heads are like filing cabinets that we cram with useful information—but also with far too many outdated materials that should be discarded. Women too readily file away myths and stereotypes that are at the very least negative and that more commonly work directly counter to their best interests.

Take the myth about college, for example, I could name countless women who have been held back from a successful career by moaning despairingly, "But I'm not a college graduate!"

Are you in this category? If so, take note of what Dr. Raymond J. McCall, professor of psychology at Marquette University, has to say: "One third of the women in the highest intelligence brackets, those with 120 IQs or above, don't go to college. Of the two-thirds who do go, half don't graduate. Therefore, two-thirds of the highly intelligent women are not college graduates."

For over eight years, Dr. McCall has been interested in speaking about these women and their rights as individuals. He feels that such women have not only the right, but the responsibility to develop professional skill to their fullest potential. He stresses that instead of making these women feel guilty about their aspirations, we should encourage them, because the United States wastes much of its talented womanpower, unlike foreign countries, as we shall see in Chapter 17.

The Doors Are There Now to Be Opened

Those who have the responsibility of staffing employee rosters are charged with getting the best available talent for filling the jobs. But up until very recent years, you could look at the management trainee positions in almost any organization and you'd find only young, white, male college graduates.

Revised Order 4 will help open doors for you, but no law or executive order can do the whole job. Why? "Prejudice against women is so ingrained it is almost impossible to make men realize it," said Rep. Martha Griffiths (D.-Mich). It was Representative Griffiths who did so much to get the Equal Rights Amendment passed.

Judge Vel Phillips, first black and first woman ever elected to the Milwaukee City Council, has often said she has met more prejudice because she is a woman than because she is black.

Rep. Shirley Chisholm (D.-N.Y.), first black congresswoman, has often said, too, "Of my two 'handicaps,' being female put many more obstacles in my path than being black." Representative Chisholm also was a sponsor of the Equal Rights Amendment, but she has said, "The law cannot do the major part of the job of winning equality for women. Women must do it themselves."

First Steps in Helping Yourself

1. Be alert to all opportunities for additional training, and don't be afraid to ask for help. Employers like to hire people who they think are interested in improving themselves.

These are some of the times that will give you an opportunity to express your interest in further training:

a. When you're interviewed for the job

b. When you are enrolled. Listen to all mention of additional training. When your supervisor has a talk with you during your first days on the job, express your interest in additional training. I realize the first few days are hectic, but still you must learn to assert your interest. Nobody is a mind reader

c. During the probationary period (three months in many firms), at the end of which the supervisor usually has a talk with new members of the staff to review progress. Express your interest in preparing for jobs ahead

d. During the annual anniversary review. Sometimes these are one-sided affairs, with the manager reviewing strong points and weak ones, but trained observers feel such reviews would be far more beneficial if the manager encouraged the interviewee to talk, too. This is one more time to see what lies ahead and how you can prepare for the future

2. Watch bulletin boards for job postings. Where there is a union, the contract spells out which jobs must be posted and the rules for this. Under Revised Order 4 there should be many job postings in years to come.

3. If there is a suggestion system in the firm, study the rules and try to make constructive suggestions that may simplify the work. For example, every firm is trying to cut down on paper work, which sometimes threatens to swamp many an office.

4. Learn all you can about the firm. As Barbara Boyle of the IBM Corporation suggested, be observant of the jobs around you.

5. Many firms have a job-evaluation system. Be sure you know what your job description is. If your duties change, your supervisor will probably talk with you first about this, but, if not, discuss it with the supervisor to find out if you are due to be moved to a higher job classification.

Here's what the Women's Bureau, U.S. Department of Labor, has to say about some common myths:

Myth: Women don't want responsibility on the job; they don't want promotions or job changes that add to their load.

The reality: Relatively few women have been offered positions of responsibility. But when given these opportunities women, like men, do cope with job responsibilities. In 1970, 4.3 million women held professional and technical jobs; another 1.3 million worked as nonfarm managers, officials, and proprietors. Many others held supervisory jobs at all levels in offices and factories.

Myth: Job turnover is higher for women than men.

The reality: Job turnover is chiefly related to job level rather than to sex. The more unskilled the job, the higher the turnover. The rate of turnover for women is not any higher than that of men in the higher-rated jobs.

Moreover, young men entering business today do not appear to have their eyes on a watch at the end of forty years! The turnover among male management trainees has been estimated as high as 36 percent. Repeated studies have shown that the average young man today may change jobs six or seven times in the course of his career. There was a time when such a man would have been regarded as a "job hopper," but no more. Now when a man changes jobs he is not looked down upon, but is more likely to be congratulated for bettering himself. The turnover among executives has been so high this has led to a whole new profession, executive recruiters, sometimes called *head hunters.*

On the whole, women who return to an office have a positive outlook. So often women say, "My work attitude now is so different from when I was a carefree teenager! Then I used every possible excuse to stay home. I had a dull job and I could hardly wait to leave it to get married. Now I really look forward to coming to work."

More Figures to Remember

There is a shortage of people between the ages of 30 and 45, because not many babies were born in the deep depression years. The big baby boom really came during and after World War II.

There is another trend which may help women like you. On many college campuses, it is fashionable to be bored. Some students disdain "the work ethic." But since business organizations are still concerned with achieving economic goals, a woman can help business earn a profit as well as a man.

Carol Kleiman wrote in "Working Woman" about a corporation that had a male sales force up until 1971. Five men sold supplies and equipment. Then the sales manager decided to assign them to selling equipment only, such as punch and binding machines. He hired five women to sell supplies, like plastic bindings, ring binders, and folders. Said Miss Kleiman:

He doubled his staff and it's paid off. The sale of supplies alone has increased 25 percent at a time when other companies are complaining about the recession.

The manager admitted he wasn't that enthusiastic to start with. "I pictured a high turnover—women getting pregnant and leaving. But not one woman has left during a period when we would have expected at least one man to." Absenteeism? No greater than the men's. Commitment to the job? Identical with the men. Three of the five women are heads of families. Training was easier. Said the manager, "The women were much more eager to learn. Since it was all brand new to them, they had no preconceived notions."

"Well trained women are good at their jobs and enthusiastic," Miss Kleiman continued. A big reason is the sales manager's attitude: women are paid exactly the same salary and commissions as men. Same benefits. He would like to hire more saleswomen, but recruitment is difficult for women suffer from the same prejudice against themselves as some employers do. Said the manager, "I had a hard time finding five saleswomen. I ran ads, but didn't get the kind of person I wanted. I needed a new receptionist, too. So I advertised and three good women answered. I hired one as a receptionist and talked the other two into joining our sales force and making more money. Were they surprised! The enthusiastic sales force is headed by the oldest, a grandmother."

Sometimes You Have to Talk Women into Trying New Jobs

The above story reminds me of this. Women believe many myths, so let's junk another one.

Myth: No one wants to work for a woman.

The reality: Many people who say this have never worked for a woman. Somehow, people have got it into their heads that in order to be a top leader you must be a tough grouch. In the first place, this isn't healthy, according to what the late John A. Schlindler, M.D., wrote in his book, *How to Live 365 Days a Year.*

Hardly a moment arises during an entire lifetime that wouldn't benefit more by a sally of humor or a cheerful lift than by a mean barb or a sharp gripe. I know executives who carry on under pressure as affably and kindly as a girl skipping down the street. They are the boys who get along and stay out of hospitals.

On the other hand, there is the great tycoon variety. They snarl and hiss and backfire, slugging everybody verbally—in short, making constant ugly asses of themselves. You do not have to envy this great tycoon type, this constantly enraged bull who paws and bellows. You may be sure he is feeling just as miserable as he sounds. In his climb up the ladder of success, he is just as miserable on the top rung as he was on the bottom rung. The added difference is that on the top rung he is dizzy with his own eminence, and that starts another immature rush of emotions that gives him, as well as those around him, a pain in the neck.

Informed sources feel that most managers don't really want to be like that.

What I know about women bosses, I didn't just read in a book. I worked for a woman, the late Coyla F. Bell, in my youth. She and her late husband, Allen C. Bell, headmaster of what was then the Bell School in Lake Forest, Illinois, worked as a team in every way, devoted to each other. They were a great pair to work for!

During the Korean war when there was a desperate nationwide shortage of supervisors, I wrote a supervisory training course for women and trained many at that time. All were women who had worked for the firm for some time, but most were timid about trying this new role. As one woman said, "It's hard to aspire to something you've been told so often you can't do." Like the sales manager just mentioned, we had to talk them into trying this new venture.

The results far exceeded expectations. It has been indeed a pleasure to see many go on to higher managerial posts, where they have supervised literally hundreds of other women. These women have received high praise from their department heads for their work. Such comments as these stand out and should encourage you:

"She is very well respected by the employees in her department because of her tactful way of handling problems."

"She is constantly adding to her knowledge of bank policies, practices, and procedures. Her knowledge of her staff's ability and the work enables her to plan ahead to the best advantage."

"Has great rapport with her staff. Able to convey information and ideas to everyone. A good listener and her staff knows this."

"All employees respect her. She is a good listener."

"Excellent in human relations. Interested in learning herself and is an excellent teacher."

What About Advancing from a Routine, Part-Time Job?

You may think, "But what chance would a housewife ever have for advancement when she comes back to a routine, part-time job?" There have been many who have advanced into supervisory and other key posts, but I'd like to tell you about one that especially illustrates my point:

When, in 1958, Dorothy Soldner applied for a part-time job three nights a week on the 10:00 P.M. to 6:00 A.M. shift, I told her she was overqualified for the job. This is something you're going to hear often if you are a college graduate, because most employers feel that a college graduate is not going to be satisfied long with routine work. Moreover, Mrs. Soldner had majored in chemistry!

However, she showed a very high aptitude for bank work on tests, and was so persistent in her desire for the job that I hired her. She wanted to work those hours because she would have no baby-sitting problems for her son who was then seven years old.

From the first she excelled in everything she undertook and did not complain about "boring work." She became a full-time supervisor in 1964, and in 1970 was elected an officer of the First Wisconsin National Bank, where she is operations officer in charge of the Reconciling Department for the Computer Center with over one hundred persons, both men and women, working under her. Mrs. Soldner said she never could have done this work without wholehearted cooperation at home because sometimes the hours are long and irregular.

Recently, Carol Kleiman wrote in *Progressive Woman* about a young black woman, Dr. Juliann S. Bluitt, new assistant dean of Northwestern University Dental School in Chicago, Illinois.

The real beauty of Dr. Juliann Bluitt is that she is a very real and warm person. To her all people are worthy of respect—students, staff, children, professional people. She looks you in the eye. She is looking for the person there. That is her real interest: *you.*

How simple life could be if we could all do as Dr. Bluitt does—

just look another person in the eye and see another human being, instead of a stereotype formed by our prejudices against people because of their sex or color!

Now that we've tossed out some of the myths that hold you back, let's look at the education you'll find on many jobs.

It would be far too lengthy to try to describe the many technical courses you'll find, such as teller training, switchboard and telephone techniques, office machine, shorthand and typing brushups. Many of you will be sent to the firm's training school before you even start your job, if you are to be a teller or a telephone operator, for example. Many of you will be trained right on the job in clerical work.

What I want to emphasize now is the hope you'll try to prepare yourselves for the *management training* courses organizations give.

Each type of business has its own *specialized* training programs for supervisors and managers. You must be *asked* to join these courses. But after you return to work, you can demonstrate that you are willing to learn, willing to work, and willing to assume responsibility.

Don't expect special treatment because you are a woman, but do expect you will be given equal opportunity if you help prepare yourself for it.

Here are some ways you can take courses, in a variety of fiields, to help yourself advance.

Tuition Refunds

As has been pointed out, many firms refund tuition paid to local universities and schools. Even big industrial companies are doing this now for women, where formerly tuition refunds were mainly for men.

Companies vary in the way they handle their tuition refund programs, but here is one way many of them operate:

Eligibility

To qualify for a refund the courses must be:

1. Approved by your supervisor or officer as related to your work, or

2. Directed toward completion of a degree which is approved by your supervisor or officer as related to your work.

Procedure

To apply for a tuition refund, some firms ask that you contact the personnel division, to get a form for this purpose. If your supervisor okays your request, he (or she) will then send a memo back to the personnel division, which will let you know of the action taken.

In smaller firms where there is a tuition refund plan, discuss your request with your supervisor, who will then take it up with the manager.

If your course is approved, pay the full amount to the school and bring your proof of payment to the personnel division, or to the designated manager in a smaller firm. You will be reimbursed for the amount of the tuition when you show evidence of successful completion of the course. Some firms refund tuition only for college courses. Others refund registration fees, tuition, and cost of books for any approved courses. The firm will let you know what is considered to be an acceptable passing grade.

Banking

The American Institute of Banking

This is one of the largest adult educational institutions in the world.

Founded in 1900, the AIB courses are available to all men and women in banks that are eligible for membership in the American Bankers Association. There are about 14,000 banks in the U.S. This figure does not include branches. Today AIB numbers 341 chapters, almost 192,000 members, and annual enrollments of more than 90,000 in classes.

"I went to work right out of high school," said Anna Foster, who became the first woman president of AIB in 1969. "I clerked in a dime store."

In 1951 she took a bookkeeping job at the Valley National Bank, one of the nation's largest. A few months after she started at the bank she began taking AIB study courses. Now Mrs. Foster is a vice-president in the Valley National Bank's commercial loan department in Phoenix, Arizona.

Mrs. Foster has this advice for women:

"As women we stand high in two qualities: we are observant and we have a special appreciation of detail. We should look around us rather than spend our time gazing at mountaintops. Let's see what the boss is doing and see if we can't do it for him."

Where interest in a particular course is limited to a small number of bankers, they may take the course by correspondence as a group under the Study Team Plan. AIB courses are also available by correspondence to individual bankers.

The AIB offers many noncredit courses and twenty-five credit courses for three certificates: the Basic Certificate, the Standard Certificate, and the Advanced Certificate. You must be a member of the AIB to take the courses, but membership fee is nominal. Banks refund the tuition and cost of books if you pass the courses satisfactorily.

National activities and benefits that are yours as a member of AIB include:

1. National public speaking contests
2. National Debate Contest
3. National awards and scholarships
4. The *AIB Bulletin,* published four times a year
5. Opportunities to hold national offices and serve on national committees
6. Opportunities to attend national conventions and regional conferences
7. Local activities where there is an AIB chapter

For further information write American Institute of Banking, Section 1, The American Bankers Association, 1120 Connecticut Avenue N.W., Washington, D.C. 20036.

Graduate Schools of Banking

There are graduate schools for executives. The Stonier Graduate School of Banking at Rutgers University in New Jersey is perhaps the oldest and best known of all, but there are many other graduate schools of banking in various regions of the country. The ones in the South were the first to admit women, and some there have always been coeducational.

The National Association of Bank Women, with a membership of over ten thousand women bank officers throughout the United States and in several foreign countries, offers twelve regional scholarships to members for one semester in a graduate banking school or specialty school (related to banking) of the recipient's choice. The association also offers a scholarship to a top woman graduate of AIB, since the organization tries to encourage young women to enter banking.

For further information about careers in banking, write Miss Phyllis Haeger, Executive Director, National Association of Bank Women, 111 East Wacker Drive, Chicago, Ill. 60601.

Many of the big banks have training schools. One of the largest banks has a course catalogue that runs eighty-seven pages! The courses run from basic typing for people who have dropped out of school to advanced management seminars, all paid for by the bank.

In case you think the best opportunities for women are in big cities, this isn't necessarily true. Many women have reached high-ranking officer status much sooner in the smaller banks.

Long before anyone thought of anything like Revised Order 4, the late Harold Brenton, president of Brenton Banks, Inc., in Des Moines, Iowa, and former president of the American Bankers Association, banking's most prestigious organization, had his own "affirmative action plan for women" in the many Brenton banks throughout Iowa.

The critical shortages of supervisors and officers during World War II led Mr. Brenton to include women in the training programs in the Brenton banks. Annually, he held a meeting at bank expense in Des Moines for all the women he employed in all Brenton Banks, from the newest file clerk to the highest-ranking women officers.

I was a speaker at one such annual meeting a few years ago. It was a real delight to observe the enthusiastic rapport between employees and management. Because they were taken seriously, all the women seemed to rise to what was expected of them in their jobs. The workshops helped them, but most of all the knowledge that the top man was genuinely interested in their progress certainly provided great motivation.

American Savings and Loan Institute

This is another very large adult educational organization. There are more than fifty-six hundred savings and loan associations in the United States. There are approximately thirty-two thousand individual members of the American Savings and Loan Institute, where it is said about twenty thousand employees enroll in the Institute's sixty-two courses.

I talked with a distinguished and enthusiastic graduate of this organization. Ardie Halyard is Chairman of the Board of Directors of the Columbia Savings and Loan Association in Milwaukee, and for many years was its managing officer. When Mrs. Halyard and her late husband, Wilbur, came to Milwaukee, in 1925, it was not easy for black persons to establish a financial institution. But they persevered, and became so well thought of in Milwaukee that a street and a housing development are named after them.

Mrs. Halyard says that every member of the staff of the Columbia Savings and Loan Association is required to be either a three- or five-year graduate of the institute. The firm pays for all training costs.

Firms vary in whether they pay the tuition at the start of the course as Mrs. Halyard's firm does, or whether they refund it. In any case, here is how the American Savings and Loan Institute helped Mrs. Halyard, who says the savings and loan business is a good one for women. ASLI offers courses in over two hundred cities where there are local chapters and study clubs. Courses are also available through the home study division if you do not live in a location where there is a chapter. Almost five thousand persons enroll in the home study courses each year.

The institute offers such courses as Introduction to the Savings and Loan Business, Teller Operations, Human Behavior, Executive Secretarial Training, Accounting, Communications, Public Speaking and Writing, Finance, Lending, Management, Real Estate, and Savings Accounts.

Membership in the American Savings and Loan Institute also provides these benefits for you:

1. Professional affiliation
2. Subscription to the *Savings and Loan News*
3. Other publications from the institute
4. Opportunities to participate in local, regional, or national institute activities
5. The opportunity to apply for admission to the institute's Schools for Executive Development or Graduate School
6. Opportunities to enroll for courses
7. Opportunities to receive Certificates of Award for successful course completions
8. The opportunity to qualify for the institute's Achievement Award, Standard Diploma, and Graduate Diploma, the most widely recognized evidence of academic achievement in the savings and loan business

For further information write to American Savings and Loan Institute, 111 East Wacker Drive, Chicago, Ill. 60601

Insurance

Another field where many women work is insurance.

In 1971 Employers Insurance of Wausau, a large nationwide firm, named a woman to head a new program designed to expand opportunities for women employees. I've met Barbara Andrews, whose job as assistant director of management and personnel development means she will implement new as well as existing educational and training programs for women to qualify for and assume positions of greater responsibility. I mention this position because as time goes on more firms will have someone like Mrs. Andrews on their staffs.

Mrs. Andrews discussed the progress of various women. One will especially interest you, a woman who returned to work at thirty-five when her four children were all in school. She had had previous experience as a legal secretary, a short period as a bookkeeper, and a year or so in a brokerage firm. Recently this woman took on a job challenge offered in the company's office claim representative program, where she and other women are declared to be outstanding successes in what were formerly thought of as "men's jobs." The former stenographer is now an assistant claim specialist, a position with a salary range of $8,500 to $12,600.

Many women in this field take courses sponsored by the following: American Mutual Insurance Alliance, 20 North Wacker Drive, Chicago, Ill. 60606.

American Institute for Property and Liability Underwriters, 270 Bryn Mawr Avenue, Bryn Mawr, Pa. 19010.

Insurance Institute of America, 270 Bryn Mawr Avenue, Bryn Mawr, Pa. 19010.

Life Office Management Association (LOMA), 100 Park Avenue, New York City, N.Y. 10017.

These courses are offered nationwide. They may be given by correspondence or in classes conducted at local vocational schools, junior or four-year colleges, or on company premises.

Employers Insurance of Wausau furnishes all textbooks and refunds tuition fees for a completed course. In those courses which require an examination fee, the fee is refunded if the student passes. In addition, an honorarium is awarded the student upon satisfactory completion of some courses. Similar refund offers are found in other insurance companies.

In addition to the insurance institutions that sponsor courses, Community Services, Institute of Life Insurance, 277 Park Avenue, New York, N.Y. 10017, publishes much free material of interest to women. This includes booklets on money management, as well as *Family News and Features,* a monthly bulletin of news, interpretation, and comment about the financial health of the family and family relationships, and articles about women going back to work and women's success in the insurance field.

Real Estate

If you get a clerical job in a real estate office, you will want to be aware that there are many courses that could help you advance in that field if you have sales ability.

I talked about prospects with Marion A. Rasmussen, president and treasurer of Marion Rasmussen, Inc., who has held posts in national real estate organizations, and who said, "I always encourage my secretary to take courses in real estate."

For further information on opportunities in the real estate field, and a list of colleges and universities offering real estate courses, write National Association of Real Estate Boards, Department of Education, 155 East Superior Street, Chicago, Ill. 60611. The *Occupational Outlook Handbook* states:

> A license is required to work as a real estate salesman or broker in every state and in the District of Columbia. All states require prospective agents to pass written examinations, which generally include questions on the fundamentals of real estate transactions and on laws affecting the sale of real estate. The examination is more comprehensive for brokers than for salesmen. In more than three-fifths of the states, candidates for the broker's license also must have a specified amount of experience as a real estate salesman or the equivalent in related experience or education (generally from 1 to 3 years). In some states, college credits in real estate may be substituted for experience.

A woman who topped the $2 million mark in sales for the second consecutive year said she loves her job, but it does mean long hours. "Selling real estate," she said, "isn't something you can do part time. I know. I tried it for four months and it didn't work. It isn't fair to the job."

A suburban home builder said, "We have practically an all-female organization today, and it happened not by accident but by design.

"We found women to be a vast, untapped pool of talent. We discovered that the successful housewife who had attained some measure of maturity was our best candidate.

"With her children raised to a point beyond where they demanded her undivided attention, we would find a woman with time on her hands and unused abilities."

A woman who is senior vice-president of this firm said that in her experience the woman of the house makes most of the home-buying decisions, and that the women on her staff are able to develop a rapport with customers because they appreciate what women look for in a house, such as walk-in lighted closets and plenty of storage space!

It isn't unusual at all any more to see women in the "million dollar club" of real estate firms.

So you never know . . . your return-to-work clerical job can lead to other things in many fields.

Special Libraries

If you work where there is a special library, this will be a great help to you in your studies. Not only will you find dozens of publications related to the business there, but many books as well. Then, too, your special library can get books for you from the public library and other sources.

In the New York metropolitan area, there are over eleven hundred special libraries. To get a complete list of them, write to Special Libraries Association, 235 Park Avenue South, New York, N.Y. 10003.

You can also ask your librarian for Kruzas' *Directory of Special Libraries and Information Centers,* published by Gale. This is a thousand-plus page volume listing specialized libraries all over the United States.

Although trained librarians head most of these facilities, library clerks are also on the staff—a job specialty that you might want to consider. Some clerks have advanced to the librarian's post after they take special courses.

Effective Listening

Some companies use a short course called Effective Listening, which was prepared by the Xerox Corporation. Others develop similar courses to suit their specific needs. Inquire about this important learning field whenever you have a chance.

Speech

By now you will have noticed how much emphasis is placed on communication in the various types of training programs. And *speech* often heads the priority list. So look for courses available to you in this field.

Dr. Peter F. Drucker, one of the country's leading business consultants, calls language skills "perhaps the most important of all the skills a person can possess. This is especially true on the job. As soon as you move one step from the bottom your effectiveness depends on your ability to reach others through the spoken or written word."

Bear this advice well in mind when you are looking ahead to the future and planning ways to help yourself advance up the ladder.

Chapter 15

How to Stand Up for
Your Rights

Time and again, you have heard women who are friends, relatives, or neighbors complain about injustices—real or imagined—in various job situations. Yet it is surprising how many women, with serious and valid complaints, fail to take any action at all, other than to gripe about being taken advantage of because they are women, or because they are new to a certain job.

You should know when, why, and how to file a complaint. Catherine Conroy, an international representative of the Communications Workers of America, has had vast experience in dealing with problems and grievances. First of all, she advises, "Keep your sense of humor. Deal with issues, not with petty things, such as saying, 'The supervisor hates me.' Depersonalize and document your complaint."

If you always wait for someone to open the door to opportunity, you may have a long, long wait. "I become so aggravated with women who shrivel up instead of speaking out," says Miss Conroy. "They're not used to telling any one but each other what they think. They must learn to tell where it counts."

And, she goes on to say, where it counts is in "moving up the chain of command until the grievance is resolved, and in making sure before starting that a dispute is a genuine grievance and not just a problem. Remember, if you work where there is a union, you must have a copy of the contract, where grievance procedures are fully outlined in it. This makes it possible for an employee at the lowest level to get the ear of management at the top should the grievance go that far.

"It's very difficult to rally women to fight for their rights through the union. They have a tendency to leave it to others. We're trying to get them to understand that this is *their* responsibility and the rewards will be more meaningful if they're involved. There are many things in union contracts that relate specifically to men and don't resolve women's problems, such as maternity leave and child care. These things have not been part of union contracts before because men didn't see the need, and they are the ones who put the contracts together. In any democratic situation, it's always more difficult because it's the vote that makes the decision, so if you don't exercise your vote, you get lost in the shuffle."

Although the union is a ready-made vehicle for women to get involved, says Miss Conroy, many do not participate as they should. And she pointed out that the men in the organization are often the ones who "wring their hands in despair" trying to get women more involved.

You will find courses and seminars and meetings that will help you in this respect. A good example was a recent nine-week course, The Role of Women in Trade Unions. The women attending the classes soon agreed that if they were to become leaders they had to qualify for the job. And they learned much about the structure of the groups in which they operated, how to overcome the personal fear of speaking publicly, how to obtain valid facts, how to argue and debate effectively, and how—if necessary—to fight with determination to achieve the objectives in which they fully believed.

Wherever you work, or find a job, whether the organization is unionized or not, be prepared to air your grievances rather than to sit and sulk about them. Normally, you should discuss problems with your supervisor first, before ballooning your personal dispute into a full-scale grievance for the attention of both union and management. The best rule is to settle the matter—to your full satisfaction—at the lowest supervisory level you can. Only if still dissatisfied should you carry it to a "higher court."

Remember, too, that the personnel department is often a place where you can easily settle a minor complaint, or at least obtain professional advice for further action. Quite often, the simple process of airing a grievance will help to solve it. Many times such a grievance is the result of a misunderstanding, which can easily be put back on balance with the help of a trained counselor.

How to File a Sex Bias Complaint

In recent years more and more women have filed complaints about sex discrimination and have, as a result, received back pay or other compensation.

Many women, unfortunately, are hesitant about filing complaints even though they may have a real one. You can get advice from your state employment service, which will direct you exactly where to go.

It would pay you to send for a booklet called "Toward Job Equality for Women" published by the Equal Employment Opportunity Commission, 1800 G Street N.W., Washington, D.C. 20506, or you may be able to get it from your state employment service. Under "How to File a Complaint of Sex Discrimination," this booklet says:

If you believe that you have been discriminated against in an employment situation on the basis of sex, you may file a charge with the Commission.

In most cases, a charge must be filed with the EEOC within a specific time after the discriminatory act took place. IT IS THEREFORE IMPORTANT TO FILE YOUR CHARGE AS SOON AS POSSIBLE.

Keep in mind that it is unlawful for any employer, employment agency, or labor organization to punish you because you have filed charges or spoken out against any employment practices made unlawful by Title VII.

After receiving your charge, the Commission will review the facts and contact you either by mail or phone you to advise you of the action it will take on your complaint. In certain states with fair employment practice laws that ban discrimination in employment, EEOC will defer investigation of sex discrimination charges to the state agency for a minimum of 60 days.

Instructions, charge forms and legal advice are available at the U.S.

Equal Employment Opportunity Commission, 1800 G. Street, N.W. Washington, D.C. 20506.

The regional offices are listed on the back page of the booklet.

The National Organization for Women has put together a kit with very *detailed* help on how to file a sex discrimination complaint, with the Equal Employment Opportunity Commission or with the Office of Federal Contract Compliance, U.S. Department of Labor, Washington, D.C. 20210. Among other things, the kit shows you how to document the evidence, gives samples of letters to write, and how to follow through.

Write to National Organization for Women, 1957 East 73rd Street, Chicago, Ill. 60649.

The cost of the kit is $5.00.

What if My Work Isn't Satisfactory?

If your work is not satisfactory, a firm should give you at least two warnings, preferably in writing. Sometimes people are unaware they are not measuring up to the standards of the job. They should always be warned so they will know the specific areas that need improving, and so they can have a fair chance to try to improve.

How to Resign

I sincerely hope that you will find a happy position in which you can have a chance to develop your talents and grow on the job. But if you should reach a point where you feel that you simply cannot stand your job another day, please do not go flouncing off as some women have done—without giving proper notice. Two weeks is considered reasonable in most organizations. You may get a temporary kick out of leaving in a huff, but the act can come back to haunt you—if you want to stay in the job market.

Try your best to cool off first, to analyze just what went wrong, and to act accordingly. Ask yourself whether you really have a valid grievance and whether you have given your employer a fair chance to hear you out.

Many firms provide an "exit" interview with all who resign from their payroll. People do not always explain their real reasons for leaving, but employers do try to learn what has gone wrong— on both sides. Sometimes an employer will send a former employee a short form to fill out after she has left. This provides space for airing one's views about the job, management, supervisors, working conditions, compensation, benefits, hours of work, and other matters. But no one is *required* either to fill out or to sign such forms. The action is strictly voluntary.

I do not want to end on a negative note by talking about severance from a firm. But, realistically, I want to point out that this does happen, and sometimes with good reason on the part of the departing employee. So, if the job just doesn't work out and you do decide to leave, think of this as an experience that may have taught you something of value. And use it as you look forward to other—and, hopefully, much better—opportunities for going back to work.

Chapter 16

Advanced Education—
Is It for You?

One of the best buys on the market today will cost you only 70 cents.

It is a book published by the Women's Bureau, U.S. Department of Labor, *Continuing Education Programs and Services for Women*. For your copy, send payment to: Superintendent of Documents, U.S. Government Printing Office, Washington, D.C. 20402. Ask for this by title, Stock Number 2902-0042, and Pamphlet 10.

This book is so packed with useful information that you cannot help benefiting from it. While waiting for your copy in the mail, ask whether the book is in your local library.

"Adult women in all parts of the country," says the book,

are seeking educational opportunities adapted to their needs and interests. In response, more and more educational institutions and related organizations are developing *special programs* for them. This report lists almost 450 programs known to be in operation in early 1971, as compared with less than 250 reported in a similar study made in 1968. These programs offered at times and in ways requested by mature women, are enabling many of them to develop and utilize untapped talents and energies.

In the book, colleges and universities are listed by state. To show you how fast the demand has grown, in 1966, only about fifteen pages were required for this listing; by 1968, seventy pages; in the 1971 edition, over one hundred pages.

The Minnesota Planning and Counseling Center for Women

These programs are not very old. In 1960, one of the first was started at the University of Minnesota when a facility was formally organized and committed to making the resources of the university more effectively useful to adult women. It is now called the Minnesota Planning and Counseling Center for Women.

The center is open to Minnesota women at all levels of education, providing advice, counseling, and information on educational and employment opportunities in the Minneapolis-Saint Paul area. It also offers scholarships, child care, job-placement service, research on women, and courses about women to undergraduates. Your best contact for information is: Mrs. Anne Thorsen Truax, Director, Minnesota Planning and Counseling Center for Women, 301 Walter Library, University of Minnesota, Minneapolis, Minn. 55455.

The program provides, through the general extension division, special short courses and liberal arts seminars for adult women. Classes are generally scheduled on a weekly basis. The program also issues a quarterly newsletter. Contact for information Mrs. Louise Roff, Director, Women's Continuing Education, 315 Nolte Center, University of Minnesota, Minneapolis, Minn. 55455.

Toddlers Go to College, Too

It is not unusual now to see small children skipping through college doors. Alverno College, a liberal arts college for women in Milwaukee, is one listed in the government book mentioned at the beginning of this chapter. Alverno provides degree courses, enrichment courses, counseling, testing, scholarship assistance, baby-sitting, and workshops for women who want to return to college or to work. I've had the pleasure of speaking at some of their workshops for mature women. One day when I came in the front door, I met a young mother and her little boy, who announced to me, "I go to school with my mother. We have lots of fun." And off he skipped to the well-equipped, well-staffed college child-care center. Unhappily, you won't find child-care centers or scholarship assistance at all the colleges listed in the government book, but there are a growing number of both.

University of Minnesota's Five-Year Report

This program has been in operation long enough to make some detailed studies. The reasons given by adult women for starting, or returning to, college indicate that vocational aspirations are much more important to the mature woman than to the adolescent girl. You may be interested in the ages of the returnees 1960–1965:

Age		Number
Not specified		5
18–22		71
23–27		358
28–32		498
33–37		516
38–42		436
43–47		313
48–52		220
53–57		108
58–62		54
63–67		18
68 plus		5
	Total	2,602

As the study reports:

The average returnee who was, or had been, married was the mother of two or three children (2.6 to be exact). Over half the mothers still had pre-school children at home at the time of their registration in the program. While some persons may deplore this tendency for young mothers to leave children, one must remember that, in most cases, a return to school is done on a very gradual basis and means only a matter of several hours per week outside the home. As long as adequate care is provided, most child psychologists do not feel that short separations of mother and child are harmful to the development of the youngster.

Why Do So Many Women Want to Start or Go Back to College?

Their reasons vary: they dropped out and now want to get a degree; they aspire to higher degrees; they want to train for jobs or brush up existing skills; or they simply have a love of learning.

"Women's interest in the classroom," says Elizabeth Duncan Koontz, director of the Labor Department's Women's Bureau, "stems largely from their growing desire to be informed participants in our fast-changing society." There they are—all ages from nineteen to women in their seventies. And what an enthusiastic and eager group! By now I guess you know I'm sold on housewives.

Good Counsel from the Minnesota Research Study

"Most mature women who are contemplating their return or first entry into the job market desperately need some realistic advice," reports the study.

They wonder if they should fib about their age, where they should begin looking for a job, what their chances are compared to those of the recent college graduate. They need an honest appraisal of the "plus" and "minus" factors and how to make the most of one and minimize the other. Although each woman is an individual case, we have found that there are several basic rules that most Minnesota Planners in search of a job have found extremely useful. Concisely stated, and without the elaboration and examples usually given these are:

1. Be honest! Realistically analyze both your good and bad points and take advantage of all the plus factors.

2. Don't limit yourself any more than you absolutely have to.

3. Use your imagination to best combine your skills and interests in a paying job during the hours you can work.

4. Be professional. Learn how to write a résumé and a letter of application, how to act during an interview, what to expect from an employer.

5. Don't expect or demand special concessions because of your age or because you're a woman.

6. Shop for a job . . . at least as carefully as you would shop for a fur coat or a new stove.

I've added these suggestions to my own counsel because sometimes when women aspire to a college degree without preparing for a specific field, they have unrealistic ideas about where they can go back to work. Other college counselors have told me this, too. Moreover, it would be misleading for me to imply that you can enter a profession such as medicine or law after you are thirty. I know some women who have attained professional degrees in middle life, but they are exceptions.

Scholarship Aid Gives Boost to Morale

There is a great deal of scholarship aid for eighteen-year-olds (who don't always appreciate it) but not much for mature women. When they receive financial assistance, the latter are likely to value it far more than many young people do.

"There was a mother of three children and wife of a precision grinder who longed to be a chemist," reported one counselor. "She took evening courses, until a ninety-dollar scholarship gave her enough faith in herself to quit a part-time job and enroll in day school full time. As a freshman in the Institute of Technology, probably Minnesota's toughest college, she came out with straight A's in physics, mathematics, and chemistry. Now the university has taken over with a larger scholarship, and she is well on her way to the career in chemistry of which she dreamed."

What's It Like to Be a Middle-Aged Co-Ed?

I talked with a woman in her forties who was a freshman.

"At first, I felt silly being in class with people the age of my children, but the kids were so nice and helpful to me I soon got over that. Often, they'd ask me to have coffee with them. Sometimes they'd tell me their problems. After I got a job teaching in junior high school, I certainly understood my pupils better, to say nothing of my own children, after being around today's youth in college."

How Important Is the Counseling?

Getting the right advice is very important. For example, today there is a scarcity of teaching jobs, whereas just a few years ago there was a drastic teacher shortage. Good counseling will help steer you away from fields that will be overcrowded. Professor Dorothy Miniace, director of the Campus Office of Continuing Education for Adults at the University of Wisconsin, Milwaukee, showed me a college booklet that anticipates many of the questions which bother adult students, be they men or women. What's more, programs like this don't leave you to sink or swim. They help you over many rough spots. So when the booklet says, "Where Do I Get the Answers? Here's Help for Adults," it really means it!

College Level Examination Program (CLEP)

"Don't forget to remind the women about the College Level Examination Program," said Martha S. Luck, dean of the evening divisions of Northwestern University, Chicago, Illinois.

Northwestern has several counselors in the evening divisions, where, among other things, they discuss CLEP. The objective of CLEP is to help people attain recognition for what they know and can do, regardless of how or where they learned it. CLEP examinations are available to anyone who wants to take them. A person can gain credit for what he knows in a certain field by taking an exam in that field and having the results sent to those colleges that recognize CLEP scores. If the score meets the standards set by the college, the person is granted college credit.

For further information write Program Director, College Level Examination Program, Box 1821, Princeton, N.J. 08540.

Always ask at the college or university where you enroll whether CLEP credits are accepted.

Women Settle for Too Little

Dean Luck has some further words for you: "Many women are underselling themselves. They settle for far too little. I firmly believe that not only does the body need exercise, but the mind does, too."

She considers night school productive for the woman who can work during the day to earn money and go to school in the evenings to insure a brighter future in her field. I can back up this advice with an excellent example. I knew a woman who was given the typical answer that she had done a good job but could go no further up the ladder because there were men with college degrees who were available for the higher positions. So she accepted the challenge, went to college for the first time in her life, earned a degree in accounting, and was ranked among the highest in her class.

I hired her!

She is now an officer of the firm, with a number of men and women working under her supervision.

Sometimes women want to return to college just for the satisfaction of getting a degree. Mrs. Luck told me about a seventy-three-year-old woman who was graduated from evening school. This graduate was encouraged to get her degree and did.

"I Live in a Very Small Town"

Many of you may be thinking that you are limited because you do not live in a city. Yet not all the colleges with counseling and special programs for adults are located in cities. And many are not listed in the government book, because truly it is almost impossible to keep up with all that have started such programs.

I talked with Mrs. Virgil Arrowood, head counselor at Hibbing State Junior College, Hibbing, Minnesota, a town of about sixteen thousand population. She gave me some interesting figures for you. For one thing, the age range for women returning to college there was nineteen to sixty-two, and the average age was thirty-three years nine months.

Said Mrs. Arrowood, "Women are returning in increasing numbers. Since we are one of the few accredited junior colleges offering an RN degree, this popular course has brought about one-half of our returning women students this school year.

"Out of 770 students, 103 are returning older women: 71 married, 14 divorced or separated, 16 single, 2 widows."

So wherever you live, if there is any educational institution around, always ask about its programs for adult students. I stress again, though, that you should try to get *counseling* about job futures, because this will save you many headaches and disappointments.

Independent Study

If you cannot possibly get to any classes, consider independent study. For example, the University of Wisconsin extension has had independent study since 1891. It offers four hundred courses and enrolls ten thousand new students annually. To get its catalogue of over one hundred pages listing courses, fees, and other data write to University of Wisconsin Extension, Independent Study, 432 North Lake Street, Madison, Wis. 53706.

To find out about other independent study courses write to your own state university or get *A Guide to Correspondence Study in Colleges and Universities* from National University Extension Association, Management Center, 900 Silver Spring Avenue, Silver Spring, Md. 20910.

Help from the Library

Libraries can be your best friends if you are working and/or going to college.

I found two useful paperback books in my own public library:

The Concise Guide to Library Research by Grant W. Morse, Washington Square Press, 1967. Price: 75 cents.

Reference Books. A Brief Guide for Students and Other Users of the Library. Compiled by Mary Neill Barton, Former Head, General Reference Department, assisted by Marion V. Bell, Head, General Reference Department, Enoch Pratt Free Library, Baltimore, Md., 1966. Price: $1.00.

Your librarian can suggest many other helpful books.

How Do Children Feel About Mom Going Back to College?

Youngsters are generally enthusiastic, when their mother seeks extra education.

"We're putting our mom through college," said the three young sons of a widow. They saved money by selling and delivering papers and doing odd jobs. They were able to provide mother with $3,500 for her education so she could find a better job and provide increased income for her family.

Said one mother of five, "When the word goes out that 'Mom's home from school,' everybody scatters to help me. Some get dinner; others help me with housework; then we all study together. We have to keep up with each other."

Some mothers report, too, that the older children take a greater interest in their own academic work. Vocational planning and exploration as a family discussion topic seems to be a natural result of mother's return to campus, according to one authority on adult co-eds.

"I wasn't back in college more than a week before I discovered that all my children could find their own mittens in the morning when all of us go to school," said one mother.

A family of seven helped celebrate one mother's graduation. "I went to college for fifteen years. Everybody helped. My husband, children, professors, and advisers all encouraged me to keep on until I got my degree."

Great Need for Lifelong Learning

Said William C. Nelson in a series of articles about the extension division of a large university:

The need for lifelong learning has never been more strongly felt than today. Statistics show that the average man will change jobs seven times. And it is predicted that half the jobs awaiting children now in third grade *do not even exist today.* We're living in a time of such rapid change that new and updated information—continuing education—is essential so that the well-educated student will not become the *obsolete adult of tomorrow.*

Lack of Direction Among America's Young Women

In its research study, the Minnesota Plan has these important words for you.

Perhaps the most important and far-reaching implications of the experiences of the Women's Continuing Education Program go far beyond the provisions needed to facilitate a return to college by mature women. While these factors smooth the way for women *motivated* to return, perhaps the larger problem is the waste of talent caused by the lack of direction among America's young women. . . . Too many young women base their plans or lack of plans on yesterday's probabilities rather than on tomorrow's possibilities. . . . Since most women expect to marry, too many parents and educators see little need for vocational planning *beyond the early years of adulthood.* In spite of predictions that the average young woman can expect to work outside the home for twenty-five years, and in spite of the fact millions of women, most of them married, are at work at any one time in the United States, the career versus marriage dichotomy is still being argued in some circles as though they were mutually exclusive categories.

Chapter 17

How Your Experience Can Help Your Family

"I wish that I'd had better counseling when I was younger and trying to plan my job qualifications for the future." How often I have heard this statement when interviewing women who want to return to work!

Although you may feel that you are having difficulties and problems in returning to work, there is an important factor here that is positive as well as negative. Your own experiences can be very helpful to others in your family, especially if you have daughters.

Theodore Roosevelt once said, "Nine-tenths of wisdom is being wise in time." I certainly go along with this, and I agree with informed sources which state that both boys and girls should be counseled as soon as they are old enough to communicate that women have the right to aim for careers of their choice.

Planning Ahead While Still Very Young

Let me tell you what I have learned while interviewing hundreds of young girls. First of all, there is the girl who is unusually bright in every way—and not just in the matter of school grades. "Are you going to college," I have asked, "or on to some form of advanced education to prepare for a lifetime career?"

"Oh, no," comes the reply time after time, "I have brothers at home who must go on to school. Girls don't really need all that education. As for me, I just want to work for a year or so before I get married."

This is all part of our traditional form of conditioning in the society that we have known. We teach men to aspire to great things. But we precondition women to hold a rather low opinion of their abilities or career potential.

Another familiar scene to me is that of the girl who is a recent high school graduate, no more than eighteen or so. "I plan to get married right away," she says. "Then I'll work until we have saved up enough money for a down payment on a car, a house, and the things we need and would like."

But the next scene comes just a few months later. The same girl, now a bride, has found out that she is pregnant. "I don't want to work any more than a few months longer," she says. "Now I'll have the baby to think about first."

And in some cases there is, unfortunately, a further development: divorce. The divorce rate for teenagers is even higher than the national rate, which is said to be one out of four marriages. Often in teen marriages there is no money. Even though the father has been ordered by the court to pay child support, many girls find it difficult to collect the payments. So the teen bride goes back to work to help support her child, while the grandmother takes care of the baby.

What can you do? Counseling must start *much earlier* than high school.

High School Counselors Can't Do the Whole Job

I've talked often with one eminent authority about this. She is Sister Mary Austin Doherty, chairman of the psychology department at Alverno College, Milwaukee, Wisconsin, who teaches a course in the Psychology of Women.

An eloquent speaker on the subject of women's rights, Sister Doherty says that one must start much sooner than high school to eliminate sex bias. "By the time girls are in high school, it's often too late to reach them. They're programmed into stereotyped roles." Like many others in the women's rights movement, Sister

Doherty feels that each woman must have the right to make her own choices and must be free to do this, without society telling her in advance what those choices must be.

"It's easier to reach girls in elementary school and college women than high school. Most receptive are women in the late twenties and early thirties. They are disappointed. They have had such a buildup about marriage and then find that they can't be continually living through someone else. They must have an identity of their own, too," says Sister Doherty.

How Some Schools Help to Break Down Sex Stereotyping

Both boys and girls get training in family living in some high schools and even in some grade schools, where they share classes in cooking, sewing, manual training, and taking care of preschoolers, to give them some idea that tots are not passive dolls but active little beings who require special knowledge to handle.

In one high school with an experimental nursery school and a home economics course, the young men liked this class as much as the girls. All learned that reading about children in a book and coping with them in their activities are two different things.

One young man said, "That room full of kids really scared me, and the children looked at us as if they were scared, too. But they soon adjusted and it was lots of fun."

I talked with Sarah A. Scott, who was then vice-principal of North Division High School, Milwaukee, Wisconsin, about this experiment. She told me how enthusiastic the students are about the class.

"Do many of the boys take cooking?" I asked.

"Oh, yes," she said, "and some take sewing, too."

"Do some girls take mechanical drawing?"

"They do, and I'd like to see more take this as basic preparation for the study of architecture."

I have noticed in my high school visits that today there are many young men in cooking classes, an enrollment which may well lead to a rewarding career. Said a top male chef, "This career can bring salaries of up to $45,000 per year, but the work isn't easy."

Some high schools now teach courses in the history of woman. As Gloria Steinem often says, "We've been reading white male history all these years." Many recognize now that women, like blacks, have been left out of a good deal of history.

And, "In the story books about medicine, why should the doctor always be a boy and the nurse a girl?" asks Elizabeth Duncan Koontz, director of the Women's Bureau.

Evidently some mothers feel the same way. In the March, 1971, issue of *Woman's Day* a mother, Marion Meade, wrote an article called "Miss Muffet Must Go—A Mother Fights Back." As she wrote, "In spite of the fact that over twenty million children under eighteen have mothers employed outside the home, you'd never guess it from picture books. They invariably portray all mothers in their domestic roles of cooks, laundresses, and cleaning women."

Mrs. Meade deplored the out-of-date, stereotyped characters and settings. She mentioned the new bibliography of good books about girls compiled by Feminists in Media and originally sponsored by the National Organization for Women, which asked sixty-five volunteers, including mothers, teachers, librarians, writers, and psychologists, to compile a list of about 250 books for readers from three to fifteen years.

To obtain this useful bibliography, send 25¢ plus a stamped, self-addressed legal-sized envelope to Feminists on Children's Media, P. O. Box 4315, Grand Central Station, New York, N.Y. 10017.

Students Should Learn Budgeting, Too

Although many young people learn the principles of economics in high school, they haven't always studied the practical aspects of money, such as learning how to budget their incomes. Many financial institutions help with this kind of training, which is especially important for those who drop out of high school or who marry upon graduation.

Some states require that consumer education courses be taught in high schools; and now that eighteen-year-olds can enter into contracts, it is even more important for students of both sexes to understand budgeting.

Parents Are Among the Nation's Top Counselors

Trained observers feel that sometimes parents may be counseling young women into overcrowded fields such as teaching or other places considered "women's jobs." Many's the time I've interviewed a young woman college graduate who majored in home economics or in education only to find she didn't want to work in that field.

"Why did you major in that subject then?" I'd ask.

"Oh, everyone said it was a good major for a girl."

For far too long, young women have been counseled out of such places as medical and law schools, and schools of business administration.

Three women business majors in Stanford University's business school organized their own recruiting system to urge more women to enroll. They called it, "What's a Nice Girl Like You Doing in a Place Like This?" In 1972, they recruited twenty-one women, sixteen more than the year before. Many young women are finding that it is better to enroll in college schools of business administration than to stick with traditional liberal arts courses.

Jobs for college graduates are becoming scarcer, a situation that is not surprising when you consider that there are presently about 9 million students in our colleges. And it has become more and more evident that a college diploma does not guarantee success in snaring a job. Many educators feel, in fact, that it is their function to educate and not to prepare students for careers, So, for the person whose objective is a career, sound counseling is vital.

College Is Not the Only Steppingstone to a Good Job

In a leaflet, "Help Improve Vocational Training for Women and Girls in Your Community," the Women's Bureau, U.S. Department of Labor, urges that more people be made aware of the new opportunities open to women. The leaflet reports that more than half of the women students are being educated in home economics, while about one-third are studying office procedures. Yet few are being prepared for industry, the trades, health occupations, or technical jobs. Yet opportunities in these areas are opening up for women, and there are some apprenticeship training programs open right now.

How Courses in Women's Studies Will Help

Sister Joel Read, President of Alverno College and a charter member of NOW (National Organization for Women) is greatly concerned about the caliber of education available to women. In October, 1971, Alverno sponsored the first conference on women's studies held in the Midwest, attracting over one hundred authorities in this field.

These educators believe that "women's studies is a legitimate academic enterprise at every level of education; primary, secondary, higher, community, continuing; including home economics, counseling education, and professional schooling such as medicine and law."

Among other things, they affirmed their support of the Equal Rights Amendment and increased executive and congressional action on behalf of all women. Especially concerned about sexist textbooks, they plan to critique them individually, make a list, and write to publishers demanding that they be revised and ask for nonsexist textbooks that eliminate bias against women.

Sister Joel Read feels that the time has come to take action against sex bias in all school textbooks and to review counseling that affects girls and women.

How Women's Rights Fits into the Counseling Picture

I believe it is important for you and your family to know more about your rights and the kinds of advice and counseling you should be receiving. The Equal Rights Amendment was passed in 1972, stating that such rights "shall not be denied or abridged by the United States or by any state on account of sex." It will greatly affect the future of all women who want to go back to work.

I, too, belong to the National Organization for Women, founded in 1966 by a handful of women with Betty Friedan as its initial president. This organization which from the first has had *male* members, has grown to over two hundred chapters with thousands of members in all fifty states. There are many other women's rights groups, too.

Some will say, "Well, when women try to get equal rights, who are among the first to put them down? *Other women!*" I cannot agree entirely with that statement. I have worked with thousands of women in business and in the National Organization for Women, and I see them learning to work together.

I cannot agree either with those who say, "Women who demand equal rights are just a bunch of frustrated fanatics."

Naturally, there are extremists in every movement, but the women I've met don't hate men, they don't want to be men, they want to work with men to make this a better world for human beings. For women they want "equality, no less; for men, equality, no more."

As many have said, "This movement is not just for women. It is part of the whole human rights program to give women, youth, blacks, and other minorities, the poor, the aged, the handicapped some voice in what happens to them."

Please note that I never use the term "women's lib." I have long been committed to equal rights for all, and I have noticed that some today use the same tone of contempt for "women's lib" that they once reserved for "nigger."

Men Can Benefit from Women's Liberation, Too

In his forthcoming book, *Beyond Masculinity*, Warren Farrell points out some of the ways men benefit.

Presently women are frequently said to "control the man" and be the "real power behind the throne." They do this controlling in ways men term cute and coy when they do not object, and devious, cunning, and underhanded when they do object. To the extent that women are the controllers of men they present a threat to men's liberty. If a woman has her own life and destiny to control, she will not be as likely to feel the need to control her husband. There will not be as much at stake in what he does because she will have her own stakes. She can approach him as an equal—someone with power—rather than as a vassal needing to manipulate the power which he possesses.

By having a life and finances and interests of her own, a woman's fear of a man's actions in the business world becomes less. He can start an interesting but risky business adventure, because if it fails, the entire world and security of a woman—her home—does not fail with it. Additionally, when the business world is not unknown and feared and the long term benefits of risks are understood his wife is not as likely to demand unrealistic "guarantees of success."

Warren Farrell is presently a Ph.D. candidate in political science and an instructor at Rutgers University, New Jersey. He has been a member of the National Organization for Women for over two years and serves on the New York chapter's board of directors. For the past several years, he has conducted consciousness-raising sessions with men, then with men and women together. He has participated in some of the IBM training for men managers mentioned elsewhere in this book.

Ms. Farrell is a team leader in the computer division of IBM, and at this writing the only woman to rise to such a position. The team she leads includes men. It sells and services computer systems for banks. Ms. Farrell is also a member of the National Organization for Women.

Others Benefit from Women's Liberation Too

As people who have worked in the labor movement know, there are always some individuals who are willing to stick their necks out to gain benefits for many. Yet often those who benefit don't realize this. Aileen Hernandez, former president of the National Organization for Women, says that many women appear indifferent to the women's rights movement. "But," says Mrs. Hernandez, "they are reaping the benefits of what we have accomplished in the past."

Take this example:

"I don't have to resign now when I'm over thirty or when I get married," said a pretty young stewardess on a talk show.

"Did you know that is because the National Organization for

Women brought suit against the airlines?" asked a NOW member on the same talk show.

Moreover, men can be flight attendants once more. Before World War II a number of airlines used stewards, but the war stopped this. After the war, the stewardesses became attractive advertising.

A few years ago, a man brought suit when an airline refused his application because of his sex. In 1972 some airlines graduated their first class of male flight attendants in years, when they pinned wings on the new stewards.

"We like to travel, too," said one of the new stewards.

And what about "my son, the nurse," or "my son, the secretary"? Some men are getting over their hangups about what was once considered "women's work." This has come full circle. A century ago only *men* were nurses or secretaries, until finally those jobs were gradually taken over by women. Now, more and more men want to go into either nursing or secretarial work. Some men feel that being a secretary is a good way to learn about the business.

"Do You Want to See Women Drafted?"

The question of drafting women into military service often arises when the Equal Rights Amendment is discussed. People who ask this either never knew or have forgotten the tremendous part American women played in World War II when *man*power was scarce. Firms not considered essential to the war industry were not permitted to hire anyone, even if they had a dozen vacancies, without permission from the War Manpower Board.

Many men who worked in offices during the day switched to war plants at night. So did thousands of women, who drove heavy trucks, operated sixty-ton cranes and became experts at welding.

Fortunately for us, thousands of women volunteered to serve in the armed forces, too. Some estimates put this figure at close to 300,000, not counting thousands and thousands of nurses. Some were killed or wounded by enemy action. Many were decorated for bravery.

These are only some of the figures that tell the story of American women in time of national peril. Most women in the equal rights movement don't favor the draft for anyone. Yet if they are needed, informed sources feel that women would be assigned duties where they could serve well, just as they did in World War II.

Interesting to recall is a statement one of the leaders of World War II made when he said, "Woman's world is her husband, her family, her children, and her home. We do not find it right when she presses into the world of man." Who said that? Adolf Hitler.

Some Ask, "Why Does the Women's Movement Discredit Housewives?"

Gloria Steinem has often said the women's movement is *not* against housewives. "If a woman examines her role and decides that is actually what she wants, her job should be recognized." Ms. Steinem advocates paying a decent percentage of the husband's earnings to the housewife.

Dr. Kathryn Clarenbach, a specialist in women's education at the University of Wisconsin, heads a new project to help women. A $65,000 grant from the U.S. Department of Labor's Employment Service will enable Dr. Clarenbach and her assistants to review and update occupations traditionally filled by women as listed in the *Dictionary of Occupational Titles*. You may recall from a previous chapter that 878 is presently the lowest possible rating in the listing. This rating includes homemaker, foster mother, child care attendant, home health aide, and nursery school teacher, among others.

One day, thanks to this grant, these jobs for women will be upgraded.

How We Compare with Other Countries

Helvi Sepila, distinguished Finnish lawyer, past president of Zonta International, and Finland's representative to the United Nation's Commission on the Status of Women, was in 1972 appointed assistant secretary general for social and humanitarian affairs at the United Nations, the first woman to be appointed to such a top-ranking job.

"The laws for centuries have been made by men," Mrs. Sepila

has said, "That women's point of view has been recently taken into consideration is thanks to political rights women have obtained in comparatively recent years. Before World War I only New Zealand, Australia, Finland, and Norway granted women the right to vote and to participate in making their countries' laws."

Finnish women were the first in Europe to be elected to parliament in 1907, the year they got the vote. Presently there are said to be forty-three women out of two hundred members in parliament. In Finland, 75 percent of the dentists are women, 30 percent of the architects, 90 percent of the pharmacists, and 25 percent of the doctors. More than 50 percent of the university graduates are women.

Mrs. Sepila says, "We are born and reared to share responsibilities with the Finnish men."

Time to Quit Joking About the Women's Equal Rights Movement

In 1971, Miss Barbara Walters of NBC's *Today Show* delivered the commencement address at Ohio State University.

She said, "It's time to quit talking and joking about women's liberation and work to improve and equalize the status of women in education, occupation, salary, property rights, and marital laws."

I agree with Miss Walters.

Naturally, there will be changes. To keep up with them, I hope you'll do your own investigating and reading and keep those clippings going into your files.

I hope you will read some of the books in the bibliography to give you more perspective on women in our history.

I hope you send for the Women's Bureau list of publications. This is your Bureau, you know. They want to help you with their many free or low cost booklets.

Someone once said there are three kinds of people in the world:

1. Those who make things happen.
2. Those who watch things happen.
3. And those who were not even aware that anything had happened.

Someone also said that leadership was marked by these things:

1. Setting a distant objective.

2. Plotting the general direction to pursue to arrive there and

3. Knowing definitely at any minute the next three steps to take.

As you read the summary of this book in the next chapter, I'm betting that you will be one who will make things happen by setting your distant objective and following up on it in the days ahead.

Chapter 18

A Brief Summation

The preceding chapters have been directed primarily at the woman who has been out of the job market for several, sometimes many years. She now wants to return to work, particularly in an office. Yet, as you have no doubt noticed, many of the subjects covered have been broader in scope, of value both to women who are seeking other types of jobs besides those in an office and to women who already have employment but feel that they should be happier in their work or making more money.

Each chapter, each topic covered, each viewpoint has been developed with *you* in mind, to offer the kind of practical realistic counsel you just cannot find in other books or even in person-to-person discussions with experts in the employment field. It would be well worth your while to review again some of the highlights that have been discussed, and especially those that apply to your particular situation or fields of interest. In my experience, when reading anything—whether a full-length book, a pamphlet, or an article or other short text—I have found it helpful to jot down notes or a checklist of the points that are of greatest meaning to me. I am certain that I have been more successful, more interested in my work and more rewarded, both financially and psychologically, than I might otherwise have been because of my practice of jotting down such notes. I urge you to do the same, not only when reviewing this book, but when reading other books and articles that provide information about jobs and job-seeking.

You will find the index that follows of value in pinpointing subjects that you might want to read about again and reflect upon at greater length. Very few people (except librarians and others trained in reference work) know the real value of an index, and seldom bother to use one. Yet if you will take about twenty seconds to turn now to the index and briefly scan the listings, you will quickly note that you can pick almost any subject in this book that you might have a question about, turn to the page referred to, and find an answer.

Don't overlook the bibliography that follows this chapter, either. In its listings you will find references to books, articles, and other texts that might be of further help to you in your job future. I have selected only readings that I *know* are practical and informative and that, for the most part, are readily available in public libraries all over the country. I have made it a point to avoid publications that are difficult to obtain, highly specialized, or that would require too much cost on your part.

Let me recap briefly some of the subjects I have covered that you might want to review again, and that I particularly want to emphasize to you. These points could form the basis for a personal checklist that would be helpful to you in seeking a job, in improving your present situation if you are already employed, or in solving some of the family and personal problems related to the woman who works and who has dependents at home.

If you are considering going back to work after a long absence from the job market, accept the fears and hesitations you may have as something normal and commonplace. Then look at the situation realistically, with the realization that you can subdue, or even eliminate, these fears by educating yourself about the current needs of employers and how you can evaluate what you have to offer. Fear, rather than being a negative drawback, can be transformed into a positive force to stimulate you to do some homework (such as reading this book) before you even begin to start looking.

Put a great big *X* mark through any feelings of guilt you may have about "taking jobs away from men who are supporting families," or running away from responsibilities to your children. I know it is easy for me to say, "Don't have feelings of guilt." But bear in mind that I do so only after having discussed this very situation with thousands upon thousands of job applicants over more than twenty years in the personnel field. More than 99 percent of the time, such feelings of guilt are completely unfounded.

Build your confidence before you apply for a job. Do this by arming yourself with as much information as possible about the kinds of jobs for which you are qualified and the current need for these jobs. And ask yourself some of the questions you may be asked in an interview, such as: "Why do I really want this job?" "What will the job mean to my family?" "What experience have I had—not necessarily in a former job—that will help to qualify me?"

Make it a point to prepare yourself with advance planning at home before you venture forth. Ask yourself what you want to be, and where you want to be, two years, three years, five years hence. Put it down on paper. And discuss each point with members of your immediate family or others who might be directly concerned. It helps to have the opinions, and assurances, of others. Yet stick to what you feel is right. Weigh opinions carefully and choose the ones that seem most realistic and constructive so that you don't end up confused and pulled in six different directions.

Prepare your résumé carefully, following suggestions made in this book and in other advance reading that you may do. A good, well-prepared résumé tells a great deal about a person. Yet keep it short and to the point. And neat. If you type, you will naturally do a good job—you *have* to if you are seeking a job that requires typing! If you do not type, have a friend prepare the résumé for you.

Give special consideration to your appearance. This includes: dress, bearing, poise, hair, makeup, and general cleanliness. It also includes your expression. You may feel flustered if you walk into an office and are greeted in a stiff, solemn voice by someone who looks as though he, or she, had just lost his last friend. But counter this with a warm smile (not a silly grin) and try to convince yourself that this is fun, a kind of game, and not a third degree. Remember that you do not have to go out and spend a great deal of money on new clothes or accessories. Simply select an outfit that is appropriate and that you feel reflects your own personality. Overdressing, to try to make an impression, can be an applicant's worst enemy. Believe me, I know. Good health is vital. So if you are sick or just plain don't feel right for an interview (other than having normal qualms), it is better to postpone it than to make a poor impression simply because you are determined to show up.

Before locking yourself into a job, make sure that you have acquainted yourself with all of the agencies and sources of information about jobs that you can. There is nothing worse than being so eager to get working that you sign up for one job, only to find out that there are many others that would have been more interesting or more remunerative. I have seen this happen again and again. In fact, when I have had the feeling that a job applicant has come to me without really having informed herself properly, I have suggested that she "shop around" a bit first. Make a checklist of sources, not only agencies but want ads, tips from friends, news items about companies and industries that are moving to your area, and similar helpful information.

If you are specifically looking for work in an office, talk to friends and neighbors who already work in offices, to make sure you know what changes might have taken place since you last held a job. Pay a visit in advance to possible places of work. You wouldn't think of buying a home or renting an apartment without looking at it. Well, there is nothing to prevent you from doing the same thing when it comes to a prospective place of work. Find a friend who works there, who will take you on a brief tour. (This is not always possible in a large organization). Or, at the very least, ask the person who interviews you if some one could show you around (assuming that the job prospects look good). Also, many large companies have plant tours to which the public is invited. If such is the case, take advantage of this opportunity to acquaint yourself with the environment in which you might be working.

If you are considering a civil service job, bear in mind that you can easily get—and are entitled to by law—detailed information on jobs. That includes specifics about places and hours of work, salary, promotions, benefits, experience and tests required, and even the outlook for the future. Federal Job Information Centers will supply everything you need to evaluate your situation. If you are looking for civil service jobs connected with local governments, you should also be able to find specific data in considerable detail.

You may be looking for a temporary position, working for

limited periods of time, either on a regular schedule or on varying schedules from week to week. If so, make sure that you understand just what a "temporary" (or "temp") does; what the term means; how it differs from full-time, regular jobs; and what kinds of benefits you do—or do not—get. I always advise people looking for temporary work to be sure to put themselves in the place of prospective employers. This is so important when you consider that you will have a variety of "employers," even though the temporary-help service is your basic employer. Consider, too, whether your temperament is right for this kind of employment. Can you shift from one to another without distraction, and without ever building a loyalty and sense of belonging to one firm?

As the time draws closer for the interview, reread everything that I have discussed in the chapter on being interviewed (Chapter 9). Do not look at this as some kind of nerve-racking confrontation or being put on the witness stand. The people who seem to come out best on interviews are the applicants who realize that this is a two-way street. Never forget that *you* are doing the interviewing, too! I know many a person in personnel who has kicked herself for not having responded well when face-to-face with an outstanding applicant who ultimately accepted a job with another firm. When I was interviewing, I myself let some excellent applicants slip away because I was not able to sell them on the job we were offering. Never be afraid to ask intelligent questions; yet avoid asking ones whose answers you should already know because they have been discussed in a leaflet or other information about your prospective employer. And please do not forget: Once you have concluded an interview which seems to have good potential, make notes of the information you received.

If you are applying for a job that requires the taking of tests, don't panic. You may say to yourself, "But I was always a very poor test taker when I was in school. I'm sure to get a low mark." Look at the test as a kind of game and prepare for it in the following ways:

1. When possible, obtain a sample test so you can acquaint yourself with the information it covers, the length, and the method used for testing.

2. Make sure that you know fully the ways in which you are supposed to answer each question, and do not be afraid to speak up and ask about any points that may be unclear.

3. Schedule test taking for a time when you are alert, well rested and in good physical and mental health.

Review salaries, potential for future income, fringe benefits, and other money matters carefully before considering any field in general or type of job in particular. Even if you are independently wealthy and it would not matter whether you made $50 or $500 a week, look at the financial side honestly and realistically from the standpoint of what you are getting for the time and experience offered. The job may be great fun—many are—but that does not mean that the salary should be any the less in relation to services performed. Make a checklist showing such details as: income from salary, remuneration in the form of benefits (especially ones like health insurance, which you would otherwise have to purchase out of pocket), tax withholding, your household budget needs, transportation costs, the increase in expenditures for clothing (which usually go up), lunch money, and similar money matters. Also, make a long-range list to determine as closely as possible how your financial situation will change in the future—and when. Consider, for example, educational needs for children or what you will want for retirement. If you are not certain of your financial ground, seek professional advice.

Lastly, bear in mind always, and repeat to yourself as often as necessary, that you as an individual must stand up for your rights— as a woman, as a person, and as part of a working team. As we all know, there are more and more agencies and organizations working to fight discrimination, chuck out the old, narrow-minded myths and customs, and restore the dignity of women to its proper place—at work as well as in the home. But *you* have a real responsibility, once you take on a job, in an office or anywhere else, to stick up for your rights and to help correct any undermining of those rights. This responsibility includes taking steps to know where to turn and what to do if you feel that there are inequities that should be corrected.

Not everything that has been discussed in this book will interest you or apply to you. That would be asking too much of an author and publisher. But please, use those chapters and passages that do apply to their fullest. Take notes, underline, make marginal jottings if you like. But do not—please do not—overlook any subject areas that can help you on the road to a satisfying job, at good pay and with an attractive future.

Good luck!

Appendix

*Directory of Federal Job
Information Centers*

Federal job information centers are open to serve you Monday through Friday, except on holidays. The best time for calling is usually between 9 and 11 o'clock in the morning and between 2 and 4 o'clock in the afternoon.

Alabama

Birmingham: In local area call 1–800–572–2970.
    Federal Bldg., Rm. 259; 1800 5th Ave. North; 35203.
Huntsville: In local area call (205) 539–3781.
    Southerland Bldg.; 806 Governors Dr. SW.; 35801.
Mobile: In local area call (205) 433–3581, ext. 237.
    First National Bldg.; 107 St. Francis St.; 36602.
Montgomery: In local area call (205) 265–5611, ext. 321.
    Arnov Bldg.; Rm. 357; 474 S. Court St.; 36104.
In other N. Alabama locations dial 1–800–572–2970.
In other S. Alabama locations dial 1–800–672–3075.

Alaska

Anchorage: The local number is (907) 272–5561, ext. 751.
    Hill Bldg.; 632 Sixth Ave.; 99501.
Fairbanks: The local number is (907) 452–1603.
    Rampart Bldg.; Suite 7; 529 Fifth Ave.; 99701.
Toll-free telephone service not currently available in other locations.

Arizona

Phoenix: In local area call (602) 261–4736.
  Balke Bldg.; 44 W. Adams St.; 85003.
In other Arizona locations dial 1–800–352–4037.

Arkansas

Little Rock: In local area call (501) 378–5842.
  Federal Bldg.; Rm. 1319; 700 W. Capitol Ave.; 72201.
In other Arkansas locations dial *–800–482–9300.

California

Fresno: The local number is (209) 487–5062.
  Federal Bldg.; 1130 O St.; 93721.
Long Beach: The local number is (213) 591–2331.
  1340 Pine Ave.; 90813.
Los Angeles: The local number is (213) 688–3360.
  Eastern Columbia Bldg.; 851 S. Broadway; 90014.
Oakland: The local number is (415) 273–7211.
  Post Office Bldg.; 215; 13th & Alice Sts.; 94612.
Sacramento: The local number is (916) 449–3441.
  Federal Bldg.; Rm. 4210; 455 Capitol Mall; 95814.
San Bernardino: The local number is (714) 884–3111, ext. 395.
  380 W. Court St.; 92401.
San Diego: The local number is (714) 293–6165.
  Suite 100; 1400 Fifth Ave.; 92101.
San Francisco: The local number is (415) 556–6667.
  Federal Bldg.; Rm. 1001; 450 Golden Gate Ave.; Box 36122;
  94102.
Santa Maria: The local number is (805) 925–9719.
  Post Office Bldg.; Rm. 207; 120 W. Cypress St.; 93454.
Toll-free telephone service not currently available in other locations.

Colorado

Colorado Springs: In local area call (303) 633–0384.
  Cascade Square, Suite 108; 228 N. Cascade Ave.; 80902.

* Refer to long-distance dialing instructions in your local phone book.

Denver: In local area call (303) 837–3506.
  Post Office Bldg.; Rm. 203; 18th and Stout Sts.; 80202.
In other Colorado locations dial 1–800–332–3310.

Connecticut

Hartford: In local area call (203) 244–3096.
  Federal Bldg.; Rm. 716; 450 Main St.; 06103.
In other Connecticut locations dial 1–800–842–7322.

Delaware

Wilmington: In local area call (302) 658–6911, ext. 540.
  U. S. Post Office and Courthouse Bldg.; 11th & King Sts.; 19801.
In other Delaware locations dial 1–800–292–9560.

District of Columbia

Metro. Area: The local number is (202) 737–9616.
  U. S. Civil Service Commission, Rm. 1416; 1900 E St.
NW.; 20415.

Florida

Miami: In local area call (305) 350–5794.
  Federal Bldg.; Rm. 804; 51 First Ave. SW.; 33130.
Orlando: In local area call (305) 894–3771.
  3101 Maguire Blvd.; 32803.
In other locations west of the Apalachicola River dial
  1–800–633–3023.
In other locations east of the Apalachicola River dial
  1–800–432–0263.

Georgia

Atlanta: In local area call (404) 526–4315.
  Federal Bldg.; 275 Peachtree St. NE.; 30303.

Macon: In local area call (912) 743–0381, ext. 2401.
  Federal Bldg.; 451 College St.; 31201.
In other northern Georgia locations dial 1–800–282–1670.
In other southern Georgia locations dial 1–800–342–9643.

Hawaii

Honolulu: In local area call (808) 546–8600.
  Federal Bldg., Rm. 104; 96813.
Toll-free telephone service not currently available from other locations.

Idaho

Boise: In local area call (208) 342–2711, ext. 2427
  Federal Bldg., U.S. Courthouse, Rm. 663; 550 W. Fort St.; 83702
In other Idaho locations dial *–800–632–5916.

Illinois

Chicago: In local area call (312) 353–5136.
  Dirksen Bldg., Rm. 1322; 219 S. Dearborn St.; 60604.
Rock Island: In local area call (309) 794–6252.
  Quad Cities Local Office; Bldg. 103, R. I. Arsenal; 61201.
Waukegan: In local area call (312) 688–4620.
  Lake County Local Office; Bldg. 3400; Great Lakes, Ill. 60088.
In other Illinois locations dial *–800–972–8388.

Indiana

Indianapolis: In local area call (317) 633–8662.
  Century Bldg., Rm. 102; 36 S. Pennsylvania St.; 46204.
In other Indiana locations dial *–800–382–1030.

Iowa

Des Moines: In local area call (515) 284–4546.
  191 Federal Bldg.; 210 Walnut St.; 50309.
In other Iowa locations dial 1–800–362–2066.

* Refer to long-distance dialing instructions in your local phone book.

Kansas

Wichita: In local area call (316) 267–6311, ext. 106.
One-Twenty Bldg., Rm. 101; 120 S. Market St.; 67202.
In other Kansas locations dial 1–800–362–2693.

Kentucky

Louisville: In local area call (502) 582–5130.
Federal Bldg., Rm. 167; 600 Federal Pl.; 40202.
In other Kentucky locations dial 1–800–292–4585.

Louisiana

New Orleans: In local area call (504) 527–2764.
Federal Bldg. South; 600 South St.; 70130.
In other Louisiana locations dial 1–800–362–6811.

Maine

Augusta: In local area call (297) 622–6171, ext. 269.
Federal Bldg., Rm. 611; Sewall St. & Western Ave.; 04330.
In other Maine locations dial 1–800–452–8732.

Maryland

Baltimore: In local area call (301) 962–3822.
Federal Bldg.; Lombard St. & Hopkins Pl.; 21201.
D. C. Metro Area: In local area call (202) 737–9616.
U. S. Civil Service Commission, Rm. 1416; 1900 E St. NW.;
20415.
In other Maryland locations dial 1–800–492–9515.

Massachusetts

Boston: In local area call (617) 223–2571.
Post Office and Courthouse Bldg., Rm. 1004; 02109.
In other Massachusetts locations dial 1–800–882–1621.

Michigan

Detroit: In local area call (313) 226–6950.
Lafayette Bldg., Lobby; 144 W. Lafayette St.; 48226.
In other Michigan locations dial *–800–572–8242.

Minnesota

Twin Cities: In local area call (612) 725–3355.
Federal Bldg., Rm. 196; Ft. Snelling, Twin Cities; 55111.
In other Minnesota locations dial 1–800–552–1244.

Mississippi

Jackson: In local area call (601) 948–7821, ext. 594.
802 N. State St.; 39201.
In other Mississippi locations dial 1–800–222–8090.

Missouri

Kansas City: In local area call (816) 374–5702.
Federal Bldg., Rm. 129; 601 E. 12th St.; 64106.
St. Louis: In local area call (314) 622–4285.
Federal Bldg., Rm. 1712; 1520 Market St.; 63103.
In other western Missouri locations dial 1–800–892–7650.
In other eastern Missouri locations dial 1–800–392–3711.

Montana

Helena: In local area call (406) 442–9040, ext. 3388.
IBM Bldg.; 130 Neill Ave.; 59601.
In other Montana locations dial *–800–332–3410.

Nebraska

Omaha: In local area call (402) 221–3815.
U. S. Court and Post Office Bldg., Rm. 1014; 215 N. 17th St.;
68102.
In other Nebraska locations dial 1–800–642–9303.

* Refer to long-distance dialing instructions in your local phone book.

Nevada

Las Vegas: In local area call (702) 385–6345.
    Federal Bldg., Rm. 1-614; 300 Las Vegas Blvd. S.; 89101.
Reno: In local area call (702) 784–5535.
    Federal Bldg., Rm. 1004; 300 Booth St.; 89502.
In other Nevada locations dial *–800–992–3080.

New Hampshire

Portsmouth: In local area call (603) 436–7720, ext. 762.
    Federal Bldg., Rm. 104; Daniel & Penhallow Sts.; 03801.
In other New Hampshire locations dial 1–800–582–7220.

New Jersey

Newark: In local area call (201) 645–3673.
    Federal Bldg.; 970 Broad St.; 07102.
In other New Jersey locations dial 800–242–5870.

New Mexico

Albuquerque: In local area call (505) 843–2557.
    Federal Bldg.; 421 Gold Ave. SW.; 87101.
In other New Mexico locations dial *–800–432–6837.

New York

New York City: In local area call (212) 264–0422.
    Federal Bldg.; 26 Federal Plaza; 10007.

Bronx: In local area call (212) 292–4666.
    590 Grand Concourse; 10451.

Brookyln: In local area call MA 4–1000, ext. 256.
    271 Cadman Plaza, East; 11201.

Jamaica: Local number to be announced.
    Marine Midland Bank Bldg., 6th Floor; 89-64 163rd St.; 11432.

* Refer to long-distance dialing instructions in your local phone book.

Syracuse: In local area call (315) 473–5660.
O'Donald Bldg.; 301 Erie Blvd. W.; 13202.
In upstate New York locations dial *–800–962–1470.
In downstate New York counties of Suffolk, Dutchess, Rockland, Orange, Putnam and N. Westchester dial 800–522–7407; in the counties of Nassau and S. Westchester dial (212) 264–0422.

North Carolina

Raleigh: In local area call (919) 755–4361.
Federal Bldg.; 310 New Bern Ave.; P.O. Box 25069; 27611.
In other North Carolina locations dial 1–800–662–7720.

North Dakota

Fargo: In local area call (701) 237–5771, ext. 197.
Federal Bldg., Rm. 200; 657 Second Ave. N.; 58102.
In other North Dakota locations dial *–800–342–4781.

Ohio

Cincinnati: In local area call (513) 684–2351.
Federal Bldg., Rm. 10503; 550 Main St.; 45202.
Cleveland: In local area call (216) 522–4232.
Federal Bldg.; 1240 Ninth St.; 44199.
Columbus: In local area call (614) 469–5640.
Federal Bldg., Rm. 237; 85 Marconi Blvd.; 43215.
Dayton: In local area call (513) 461–4830, ext. 5540.
Grant-Deneau Bldg., Rm. 610; 40 W. Fourth St.; 45402.
In other northern Ohio locations dial 1–800–362–2910.
In other southern Ohio locations dial *–800–762–2435.

Oklahoma

Oklahoma City: In local area call (405) 231–4948.
210 NW Sixth St.; 73102.
In other Oklahoma locations dial 1–800–522–3781.

* Refer to long-distance dialing instructions in your local phone book.

Oregon

Portland: In local area call (503) 221–3141.
   Multnomah Bldg., Lobby; 319 SW. Pine St.; 97204.
In other Oregon locations dial *–800–452–4910.

Pennsylvania

Harrisburg: In local area call (717) 782–4494.
   Federal Bldg., Rm. 168; 17108.
Philadelphia: In local area call (215) 597–7440.
   128 N. Broad St.; 19102. (After May, 1973: Federal Bldg.;
   6th & Market Sts.; 19106.)
Pittsburgh: In local area call (412) 644–2755.
   Federal Bldg.; 1000 Liberty Ave.; 15222.
In other eastern Pennsylvania locations dial 1–800–462–4050.
In other central and western Pennsylvania locations dial 1–800–
   242–0588.

Puerto Rico

San Juan: The local number is (809) 765–0404, ext. 209.
   Pan Am Bldg.; 255 Ponce de Leon Ave.; Hato Rey, P. R. 00917.
Toll-free telephone service is not available from other locations.

Rhode Island

Providence: The local number is (401) 528–4447.
   Federal and Post Office Bldg., Rm. 310; Kennedy Plaza; 02903.
Toll-free telephone service not currently available from other
locations.

Southern Carolina

Charleston: In local area call (803) 577–4171, ext. 328.
   Federal Bldg.; 334 Meeting St.; 29403.

  * Refer to long-distance dialing instructions in your local phone book.

Columbia: In local area call 1–800–922–3790.
Main Post Office Bldg., Rm. 426; 29201.
In other South Carolina locations dial 1–800–922–3790.

South Dakota

Rapid City: In local area call (605) 348–2221.
Dusek Bldg., Rm. 118; 919 Main St.; 57701.
In other South Dakota locations dial *–800–742–8944.

Tennessee

Memphis: In local area call (901) 534–3956.
Federal Bldg.; 167 N. Main St.; 38103.
In other Tennessee locations dial 1–800–582–6291.

Texas

Corpus Christi: In local area call (512) 883–5511, ext. 362.
Downtown Postal Station, Rm. 105; 701 N. Upper Broadway;
78401.
Dallas: In local area call (214) 749–3156.
Rm. 1C42; 1100 Commerce St.; 75202.
El Paso: In local area call (915) 533–9351, ext. 5388.
National Bank Bldg.; 411 N. Stanton St.; 79901.
Fort Worth: In local area call (817) 334–3484.
819 Taylor St.; 76102.
Houston: In local area call (713) 226–5501.
702 Caroline St.; 77002.
San Antonio: In local area call (512) 225–5511, ext. 4343.
Post Office and Courthouse Bldg.; 615 E. Houston St.; 78205.
In other northern Texas locations dial 1–800–492–4400.
In other Gulf Coast Texas locations dial 1–800–392–4970.
In other south central Texas locations dial 1–800–292–5611.
In other western Texas locations dial *–800–592–7000.

* Refer to long-distance dialing instructions in your local phone book.

Utah

Ogden: In local area call (801) 399–6854.
   Federal Bldg., Rm. 1413, 324 25th St., 84401.
Salt Lake City: In local area call (701) 524–5744.
   Federal Bldg. Annex; 135 S. State St.; 84111.
In other Utah locations dial 1–800–662–5355.

Vermont

Burlington: In local area call (802) 862–6501, ext. 259.
   Federal Bldg., Rm. 317; Elmwood Ave. & Pearl St.; 05401.
In other Vermont locations dial 1–800–642–3120.

Virginia

Norfolk: In local area call (703) 625–6515.
   415 St. Paul's Blvd.; 23510.
Richmond: In local area call (703) 782–2732.
   Federal Bldg., 400 N. Eighth St.; 23240.
D. C. Metro Area: In local area call (202) 737–9616.
   U. S. Civil Service Commission, Rm. 1416; 1900 E St. NW;
   20415.
In other Virginia locations dial *–800–582–8171.

Washington

Seattle: In local area call (206) 442–4365.
   Federal Bldg.; First Ave. & Madison St.; 98104.
Spokane: In local area call (509) 446–2536.
   U. S. Post Office, Rm. 200; 904 Riverside; 99210.
Tacoma: In local area call (206) 627–1700.
   Washington Bldg., Rm. 610; 1019 Pacific Ave.; 98402.
Vancouver: The local number is 693–0541.
In other Washington locations dial *–800–552–0714.

   * Refer to long-distance dialing instructions in your local phone book.

West Virginia

Charleston: In local area call (304) 343–6181, ext. 226.
    Federal Bldg.; 500 Quarrier St.; 25301.
In other West Virginia locations dial *–800–642–9027.

Wisconsin

Milwaukee: In local area call (414) 224–3761.
    Plankinton Bldg., Rm. 205; 161 W. Wisconsin Ave.; 53203.
In other Wisconsin locations dial *–800–242–9191.

Wyoming

Cheyenne: In local area call (307) 778–2220, ext. 2108.
    Teton Bldg., Rm. 108; 1805 Capitol Ave.; 82001.
In other Wyoming locations dial 1–800–442–2766.

* Refer to long-distance dialing instructions in your local phone book.

Sample of Civil Service Test Given to Typists and Stenographers

The following sample questions show the types of questions that will be found in the written test. They show also how the questions in the test are to be answered. Read the directions below; then answer the sample questions. Record your answers on the Sample Answer Sheet on these pages.

Each question has several suggested answers lettered A, B, C, etc. Decide which one is the best answer to the question. On the Sample Answer Sheet, find the answer space numbered the same as the question and darken the space lettered the same as the best suggested answer. Then compare your answers with the answers given in the Correct Answers to Sample Questions.

Sample Questions 1 through 5—*Verbal Abilities*

1. *Previous* means most nearly
   A) abandoned   C) timely
   B) former   D) younger

2. (*Reading*) "Just as the procedure of a collection department must be clear cut and definite, the steps being taken with the sureness of a skilled chess player, so the various paragraphs of a collection letter must show clear organization, giving evidence of a mind that, from the beginning, has had a specific end in view."

   The quotation best supports the statement that a collection letter should always
   A) show a spirit of sportsmanship
   B) be divided into several paragraphs
   C) be brief, but courteous
   D) be carefully planned

   In the following question, the first two words in capital letters go together in some way. The third word in capital letters is related in the same way to one of the words lettered A, B, C, or D.

3. SPEEDOMETER is related to POINTER as WATCH is related to
   A) case   C) dial
   B) hands   D) numerals

   Find the correct spelling of the word and darken the proper answer space. If no suggested spelling is correct, darken space D.

4. A) athalete   C) athlete
   B) athelete   D) none of these

   Decide which sentence is preferable with respect to grammar and usage suitable for a formal letter or report

5. A) They do not ordinarily present these kind of reports in detail like this.
   B) A report of this kind is not hardly ever given in such detail as this one.
   C) This report is more detailed than what such reports ordinarily are.
   D) A report of this kind is not ordinarily presented in as much detail as this one is.

Sample Questions 6 through 8—*Arithmetic*

Work each problem and compare your answer with suggested answers A, B, and C. If your answer does not agree with any of these suggested answers, darken space D.

             Answers

6. Subtract:
       2 1 9
   − 1 1 0
                 A) 99
                 B) 109
                 C) 199
                 D) none of these

7. Add:
   $5.2 + .96 + 47.0 =$
                 A) 19.5
                 B) 48.48
                 C) 53.16
                 D) none of these

8. 47% of $538 =$
                 A) 11.45
                 B) 252.86
                 C) 285.14
                 D) none of these

Sample Answer Sheet

	A	B	C	D	E
1					
2					
3					
4					
5					
6					
7					
8					

Correct Answers to Sample Questions

	A	B	C	D	E
1		■			
2				■	
3		■			
4			■		
5				■	
6		■			
7			■		
8		■			

Sample Questions 9 through 30—*Clerical Aptitude*

Sample questions 9 through 13 require name and number comparisons.   In each line across the page there are three names or numbers that are much alike.   Compare the three names or numbers and decide which ones are exactly alike.   On the Sample Answer Sheet at the right, mark the answer—

A   if ALL THREE names or numbers are exactly ALIKE
B   if only the FIRST and SECOND names or numbers are exactly ALIKE
C   if only the FIRST and THIRD names or numbers are exactly ALIKE
D   if only the SECOND and THIRD names or numbers are exactly ALIKE
E   if ALL THREE names or numbers are DIFFERENT

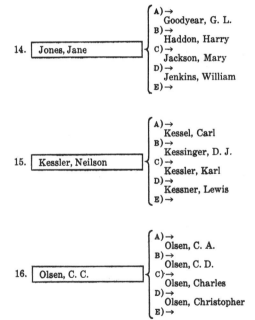

9.   Davis Hazen   David Hozen   David Hazen
10. Lois Appel   Lois Appel   Lois Apfel
11. June Allan   Jane Allan   Jane Allan
12. 10235   10235   10235
13. 32614   32164   32614

In the next group of sample questions, there is a name in a box at the left, and four other names in alphabetical order at the right.   Find the correct space for the boxed name so that it will be in alphabetical order with the others, and mark the letter of that space as your answer.

14. | Jones, Jane |
    A) →
      Goodyear, G. L.
    B) →
      Haddon, Harry
    C) →
      Jackson, Mary
    D) →
      Jenkins, William
    E) →

15. | Kessler, Neilson |
    A) →
      Kessel, Carl
    B) →
      Kessinger, D. J.
    C) →
      Kessler, Karl
    D) →
      Kessner, Lewis
    E) →

16. | Olsen, C. C. |
    A) →
      Olsen, C. A.
    B) →
      Olsen, C. D.
    C) →
      Olsen, Charles
    D) →
      Olsen, Christopher
    E) →

Sample Answer Sheet

	A	B	C	D	E
9					
10					
11					
12					
13					
14					
15					
16					

Correct Answers to Sample Questions

	A	B	C	D	E
9					■
10		■			
11				■	
12	■				
13			■		
14					■
15				■	
16		■			

In the following questions, do whatever the question says, and find your answer among the list of suggested answers for that question. Mark the Sample Answer Sheet A, B, C, or D, for the answer you obtained; or if your answer is not among these, mark E for that question.

17. Add:

$$\begin{array}{r} 2\ 2 \\ +\ 3\ 3 \\ \hline \end{array}$$

Answers
A) 44 B) 45
C) 54 D) 55
E) none of these

19. Multiply:

$$\begin{array}{r} 2\ 5 \\ \times\ 5 \\ \hline \end{array}$$

Answers
A) 100 B) 115
C) 125 D) 135
E) none of these

18. Subtract:

$$\begin{array}{r} 2\ 4 \\ -\ 3 \\ \hline \end{array}$$

A) 20 B) 21
C) 27 D) 29
E) none of these

20. Divide:

$$6\ \overline{\smash)\ 1\ 2\ 6}$$

A) 20 B) 22
C) 24 D) 26
E) none of these

There is a set of 5 suggested answers for each group of sample questions that appears below. Do not try to memorize these answers, because there will be a different set on each page in the test.

To find the answer to each question, find which one of the suggested answers contains numbers and letters all of which appear in that question. These numbers and letters may be in any order in the question, but all four must appear. If no suggested answer fits, mark E for that question.

21. 8 N K 9 G T 4 6

22. T 9 7 Z 6 L 3 K

23. Z 7 G K 3 9 8 N

24. 3 K 9 4 6 G Z L

25. Z N 7 3 8 K T 9

26. 2 3 P 6 V Z 4 L

27. T 7 4 3 P Z 9 G

28. 6 N G Z 3 9 P 7

29. 9 6 P 4 N G Z 2

30. 4 9 7 T L P 3 V

Suggested Answers
A=7, 9, G, K
B=8, 9, T, Z
C=6, 7, K, Z
D=6, 8, G, T
E=none of these

Suggested Answers
A=3, 6, G, P
B=3, 7, P, V
C=4, 6, V, Z
D=4, 7, G, Z
E=none of these

Sample Answer Sheet

Correct Answers to Sample Questions

All Stenographer and Typist competitors will take a typing test (Plain Copy). The sample given below shows the kind of material that competitors must copy. See whether you can copy it once in 5 minutes and how many errors your copy contains. Competitors will be required to meet a certain minimum in accuracy as well as in speed. Above the minimum speed and accuracy requirements, accuracy counts twice as much as speed in determining whether the competitor is eligible on typing.

Space, paragraph, spell, punctuate, capitalize, and begin and end each line precisely as shown in the exercise.

In the examination you will have 5 minutes in which to make copies of the test exercise, keeping in mind that your eligibility will depend upon accuracy as well as speed. When you complete the exercise, simply double space and begin again.

You must type more than 16 lines to be eligible in speed. With that minimum speed, your paper should not have more than 3 errors. The number of errors permitted increases with the amount typed. Higher standards will be required for the higher grades.

```
         This practice exercise is similar in length and diffi-
    culty to the one that you will be required to typewrite for
    the Plain Copy Test. You are to space, capitalize, punctu-
    ate, spell, and begin and end each line precisely as in the
    copy. Directions regarding erasures will be given when you
    take the Plain Copy Test. Follow carefully all directions
    given at the time of the examination. Practice typewriting
    this material on scratch paper until the examiner tells you
    to stop, remembering that for this examination it is more
    important to typewrite accurately than to typewrite rapidly.

         There are several ways in which a typist can prepare
    herself to be an efficient worker in a business office.
    First of all, she should know her typewriter thoroughly, the
    location of all the keys, even those used infrequently, and
    the use of the marginal stops and extra devices furnished on
    modern typewriters. In addition to being completely familiar
    with the typewriter, she should be equipped with knowledge
    of the correct spellings and correct use of a large number
    of words. Although a letter has been typewritten neatly,
    without omissions or insertions, it will still be considered
    unsatisfactory if it contains any misspellings whatsoever.
```

Only Stenographer competitors take a stenography test. **The sample** below shows the **length of** material dictated. Have someone dictate the passage to you so that you can see how well prepared you are to take dictation at 80 words a minute. Each pair of lines is dictated in 10 seconds. Dictate periods, but not commas. Read the exercise with the expression the punctuation indicates.

In recent years there has been a great increase in the need for capable stenographers,	10 sec.
not only in business offices but also in public service agencies, both	20 sec.
governmental and private. (Period) The high schools and business schools in many parts of	30 sec.
the country have tried to meet this need by offering complete commercial courses. (Period)	40 sec.
The increase in·the number of persons who are enrolled in these courses shows that	50 sec.
students have become aware of the great demand for stenographers. (Period) A person	1 min.
who wishes to secure employment in this field must be able to take dictation	10 sec.
and to transcribe the notes with both speed and accuracy. (Period) The rate of	20 sec.
speed at which dictation is given in most offices is somewhat less than that of	30 sec.
ordinary speech. (Period) Thus, one who has had a thorough training in shorthand	40 sec.
should have little trouble in taking complete notes. (Period) Skill in taking dictation	50 sec.
at a rapid rate is of slight value if the stenographer cannot also type her notes	2 min.
in proper form. (Period) A businessman sometimes dictates a rough draft of the ideas	10 sec.
he wishes to have included in a letter, and leaves to the stenographer the task	20 sec.
of putting them in good form. (Period) For this reason, knowledge of the essentials	30 sec.
of grammar and of composition is as important as the ability to take	40 sec.
dictation. (Period) In addition, a stenographer should be familiar with the sources of	50 sec.
general information that are most likely to be used in office work. (Period)	3 min.

On page 6, the TRANSCRIPT and WORD LIST for part of the above dictation are similar to those each competitor will receive for the dictation test. Many words have been omitted from the TRANSCRIPT. Compare your notes with it. When you come to a blank space in the TRANSCRIPT, decide which word (or words) belongs in the space. Look for the missing word in the WORD LIST. Notice what letter is printed beside the word. Write that letter in the blank. *c* is written in blank 1 to show how you are to record your choice. Write *E* if the exact answer is NOT in the WORD LIST. *You may also write the word (or words) or the shorthand for it, if you wish.* The same choice may belong in more than one blank.

ALPHABETIC WORD LIST

Write E if the answer is NOT listed.

advertising—A	many—D
agencies—D	marked—A
almost—C	met—A
also—C	most—C
and—D	need—D
business—B	offering—D
but—A	only—B
claimed—B	opening—A
colleges—C	parts—A
complete—B	private—C
country—A	schools—D
demand—B	sections—B
especially—D	the need—A
even—B	their—D
government—B	there—C
great—C	to complete—C
has been—D	to meet—C
high schools—A	to offer—B
in—C	trained—C
in government—A	tried—A

TRANSCRIPT

In recent years ___ *C* ___ ___ a ___
                    1   2   3

increase ___ ___ for ___ stenographers,
          4   5   6

not ___ ___ ___ offices ___ ___
     7   8   9   10   11

in public ___ ___, both ___ and
           12   13   14

___. The ___ and business ___
 15   16   17

in ___ ___ ___ ___ have
    18   19   20   21

___ ___ this need by ___ ___
 22   23   24   25

commercial courses. . . .

(For the next sentences there would be another word list, if the entire sample dictation were transcribed.)

You will be given an answer sheet like the sample at the left, below, on which your answers can be scored by machine. Each number on the answer sheet stands for the blank with the same number in the transcript. Darken the space below the letter that is the same as the letter you wrote in the transcript. If you have not finished writing letters in the blanks in the transcript, or if you wish to make sure that you have lettered them correctly, *you may continue to use your notes after you begin marking the answer sheet.*

Answer Sheet for Sample Transcript

Correct Answers for Sample Transcript

Bibliography

GENERAL

Bird, Caroline, with Briller, Sara Welles. *Born Female: The High Cost of Keeping Women Down.* Rev. ed. New York: David McKay Co., 1970.

Chisholm, Shirley. *Unbought and Unbossed.* Boston: Houghton Mifflin, 1970.

Cross, Wilbur. *A Job with a Future in Computers.* New York: Grosset & Dunlap, 1969.

Daly, Mary. *The Church and the Second Sex.* New York: Harper & Row, 1968.

de Beauvoir, Simone. *The Second Sex.* 1952; New York: Bantam Books, 1961.

———. *The Coming of Age.* New York: Putnam, 1972. (A definitive study of the universal problem of growing old.)

DeCrow, Karen. *A Young Woman's Guide to Liberation.* New York: The Bobbs-Merrill Co., 1971.

Flexner, Eleanor. *Century of Struggle. The Women's Rights Movement in the United States.* New York: Atheneum, 1970.

———. *Women's Rights—Unfinished Business.* Public Affairs Pamphlet, 381 Park Avenue South, New York, N.Y. 10016. 25¢

Friedan, Betty. *The Feminine Mystique.* New York: W. W. Norton & Co., 1963. (Ms. Friedan writes a column, "Betty Friedan's Notebook," which is published in *McCall's.*)

Janeway, Elizabeth. *Man's World, Woman's Place: A Study in Social Mythology.* New York: William Morrow & Co., 1971.

Mill, John Stuart. *On the Subjection of Women.* 1869, 1912: Oxford U. Press, New York. (with *On Liberty and Representative Government*.)

Mindey, Carol. *Divorced Mother, A Guide to Readjustment*. New York: McGraw-Hill, 1970.

Montagu, Ashley. *The Natural Superiority of Women*. New York: The Macmillan Co., 1952.

Nye, F. I., and Hoffman, L. W. *The Employed Mother in America*. Chicago: Rand McNally & Co., 1963.

Pogrebin, Letty Cottin. *How to Make It in a Man's World*. New York: Doubleday & Co., 1970. (Ms. Pogrebin writes a column called "The Working Woman" in *The Ladies' Home Journal*.)

Poor, Riva M. *4 Days, 40 Hours: Reporting a Revolution in Work and Leisure*. Cambridge, Mass.: Bursk & Poor, 1971.

Sarnoff, Dorothy. *Speech Can Change Your Life*. New York: Doubleday & Co., 1970.

Scott, Anne Firor. *The Southern Lady, from Pedestal to Politics*. Chicago: University of Chicago Press, 1970.

Taves, Isabella. *Women Alone*. New York: Funk & Wagnalls, 1968.

Thompson, Mary Lou, ed. *Voices of the New Feminism*. Boston: Beacon Press, 1970.

Walters, Barbara. *How to Talk with Practically Anybody About Practically Anything*. New York: Doubleday & Co., 1970.

Woolf, Virginia. *A Room of One's Own*. New York: Harbinger Books, 1929.

The Women's Bureau, U.S. Department of Labor, is dedicated to helping you, and has many booklets that will do that. Founded on June 5, 1920, the Women's Bureau was charged with the "responsibility to formulate standards and policies which shall promote the welfare of wage-earning women, improve their working conditions, increase their efficiency, and advance their opportunities for profitable employment."

To obtain the list, *Publications of the Women's Bureau* (Leaflet 10), write Women's Bureau, Workplace Standards Administration, U.S. Department of Labor, Washington, D.C. 20210. The booklets are free or available at low cost. The addresses of the regional offices of the Women's Bureau are listed in the leaflet.

MONEY AND CONSUMER EDUCATION

Blair, Lorraine L. *Answers to Your Everyday Money Questions.* Chicago: Henry Regnery Co., 1968.

Simons, Gustave. *What Every Woman Doesn't Know.* New York: The Macmillan Co., 1964. (Mr. Simons, a well-known tax lawyer, discusses financial, work, and tax problems, among others.)

Some Better Business Bureau publications:

Facts on Computer Careers. Council of Better Business Bureaus, Inc., 1972. 1150 17th St. N.W., Washington, D.C. 20036, in cooperation with American Federation of Information Processing Societies, 210 Summit Avenue, Montvale, N.J. 07645.

Tips on Work at Home Schemes. Publication Number 204. Council of Better Business Bureaus, Inc., 1972. 1150 17th St. N.W., Washington, D.C. 20036.

Sylvia Porter's column, syndicated in 350 papers. (Miss Porter is a leading financial writer who sets out to translate what she calls economic "bafflegab" into English and understandable consumer education. She says her formula is "Here is what is going on and here is what you can do to protect yourself." Miss Porter also writes a column, "Spending Your Money," published monthly in *The Ladies' Home Journal.*)

Some Public Affairs Pamphlets on consumer education and handling money (on sale at some libraries, or write to Public Affairs Pamphlets, 381 Park Avenue South, New York, N.Y. 10016):
Margolius, Sidney. *Family Money Problems.* No. 412 (1967). 25¢
———. *How to S-t-r-e-t-c-h Your M-o-n-e-y.* No. 302A (1970). 25¢
———. *The Responsible Consumer.* No. 453 (1970). 25¢

SOME HELP WITH THE HOUSE

Curry, Barbara A. *Okay, I'll Do It Myself! Or a Handywoman's Primer That Takes the Mystique Out of Home Repairs.* New York: Random House, 1972.

Laird, Jean E. *Around the House Like Magic*. New York: Harper & Row, 1967.

Also:

"Career Counseling: New Perspectives for Women and Girls," is an annotated bibliography published by the Business and Professional Women's Foundation, 2012 Massachusetts Avenue N.W., Washington, D.C. 20036. 50 cents per copy.

Jack and Jill ("This is the world that Jack built . . . and Jill came tumbling after") is a booklet for teachers, counselors, community organizations, parents, and students aimed at arousing awareness of sex-role stereotyping in all phases of life. Copies available for $1.00 from Bonnie Zimmerman, 36 Castledown Rd., Pleasanton, California 94566. Published by the Status of Women Committee, California State Division, American Association of University Women.

Women and the Law: The Unfinished Revolution by Leo Kanowitz. Albuquerque: University of New Mexico Press, 1969. Talks about employment, divorce, rights of single and married women, and more.

Index

Index